You Only Have to Ask!

The priorities and values of Gen Z, who are now entering the workplace, are not always aligned with the priorities and values of earlier generations. Gen Z are viewed as fundamentally different from those who have gone before and by 2025, they will make up 30% of the workplace. Understanding the needs and expectations of Gen Z will highlight how today's managers and leaders can support them performing to their full potential.

You Only Have to Ask!: How to Realise the Full Potential of Gen Z at Work explores the ever-evolving dynamic of the employer–employee relationship and provides guidance on how to navigate this successfully. The book highlights the need for today's leaders to appreciate and adapt to the opportunities for increased levels of satisfaction, greater committed participation and fresh energy that Gen Z are able and willing to bring to the workplace. This means creating a culture that engages the minds and commitment of this new generation whose expectations and needs may not always conform to traditional management practice.

The book also provides a "pick and mix" framework to help elevate the communication between managers and teams that can be applied immediately. When using this framework, every performer can develop and measure the level of engagement—in both the team and themselves—thus creating the ultimate environment in which everyone is enabled to do their best work.

The eight questions in this book hold the key to a customised, dynamic, supportive environment for personal, team and business growth and future success.

You Only Have to Ask!

How to Realise the Full Potential of Gen Z at Work

Anna Hislop and Peter Lightfoot

Routledge
Taylor & Francis Group

A PRODUCTIVITY PRESS BOOK

First published 2024
by Routledge
605 Third Avenue, New York, NY 10158

and by Routledge
4 Park Square, Milton Park, Abingdon, Oxon, OX14 4RN

Routledge is an imprint of the Taylor & Francis Group, an informa business

© 2024 Anna Hislop and Peter Lightfoot

ISBN: 9781032757797 (hbk)
ISBN: 9781032715353 (pbk)
ISBN: 9781003475613 (ebk)

DOI: 10.4324/9781003475613

Typeset in Trade Gothic LT Std
by Newgen Publishing UK

To bewildered* business managers and team leaders, everywhere.

*Bewilderment: ... fundamental to the search for insight. It is a necessary first step in the effort to get to a point of greater clarity and to see the right way even when—especially when—it seems to be lost.

Contents

About the Authors

There are few professionals in the UK who know more about the expectations and potential of Gen Z than **Anna Hislop**. As a schoolteacher in her native Sweden, she felt compelled to adapt her usual teaching style in order to meet the learning needs of a new generation of students. She noticed that they saw the challenges and opportunities that the world offered them in a totally different, more independent, way. As she progressed in her role within school leadership and interacted with Gen Z students, with their parents and with school policymakers, she gained a deeper understanding of their unique circumstances and motivations.

Now, in the UK, working as a successful leadership coach, her clients are becoming aware that these same young, energised, well-educated and tech-savvy-free thinkers are entering the workplace. The challenge is that they seem less readily responsive to being "managed" in a traditional way.

In this book she shares all her experience working with Gen Z and today's leaders, across industries and regions, helping them to create harmonious and successful workplace environments. In such a workplace, Gen Z can thrive and contribute enormously to achieving business goals as well as their own personal learning and growth.

Peter Lightfoot was a business coach when the concept of coaching was applied only to sports. He worked closely with Sir John Whitmore, who was a pioneer of coaching in the workplace and whose book *Coaching for Performance*[1] has sold over a million copies.

Peter has vast experience in helping managers and team leaders, in large and small companies, to coach their own teams to greater effectiveness and success. His approach to learning and performance can apply to everyone in the workplace and equally to Gen Z and future generations!

His coaching techniques, which have enabled many leaders and managers to inspire others, have provided our framework for this book. This framework offers, to anyone responsible for developing the skills and commitment of their own teams, a way of supporting every generation to achieve the results that business demands.

Together, Anna and Peter combine their knowledge and experience to create a more optimistic and prosperous future in the workplace. They highlight the opportunities that arise from Gen Z's fresh perspectives and expectations, showcasing the valuable contributions they bring to employers and colleagues alike.

---

1 Whitmore, J. (2009). *Coaching for Performance: Growing Human Potential and Purpose: The Principles and Practice of Coaching and Leadership*. 4th Edition, Nicholas Brealey, London.

Acknowledgements

Anna Hislop

To Alex and to the classes of 2010–2019, my remarkable Gen Z students, and current emerging leaders and talents. Their insight, courage and determination to play their own game, in both work and life, are truly inspirational.

Peter Lightfoot

Sir John Whitmore, author of *Coaching for Performance*, who together with David Whitaker and David Hemery were founders of Performance Consultants and past colleagues; Professor Alan Beggs, Tony Gillan, Timothy Gallwey, founder of the Inner Game Institute, John Shedden, Ali Ross, The English Ski Council (now Snowsport England) and Edwina. All those whose wisdom, enthusiasm and support contributed so much to my love of coaching in both sport and business…

Introduction

I thought I was an effective manager, getting good results. But I'm now working harder than ever and feeling more and more stressed, and my team seems unengaged, as if they lack the passion and drive to go the extra mile.

Surveys on employees' satisfaction, motivation and engagement are telling us a depressing story. Just over 20% of employees, and that includes Gen Z,[1] feel fully engaged at work. In Europe the number is only 13%.[2] These numbers highlight a gap between the stimulating workplace that each employee expects and deserves and the environment in which they find themselves actually working.

In many companies, maybe yours, that gap is getting wider each year. Traditional management practices will never reduce it. The frustration of managers and team leaders will only increase.

The surveys tell us why. Younger generations, especially Gen Z, expect more from their workplace than a salary and steady career advancement. Unless they feel fully supported, valued and involved, they will unconsciously begin to resist top-down orthodoxy, avoid contributing original ideas and minimise their efforts. Businesses will start to stagnate as the brightest and best will be looking to leave, and the

---

1 The abbreviation Gen Z is used throughout the book.
2 GALLUP (2024) gallup.com accessed 01-10-2023 available at www.gallup.com/workplace/349
484/state-of-the-global-workplace.aspx

work satisfaction for those left behind becomes a distant dream.

But it doesn't have to be like that. "You Only Have To Ask!" offers you a framework of questions that lead to better understanding and a closing of the gap. Perhaps you are asking some of these questions of yourself? Each member of your team and department is certainly asking them. Right now! They have their own answers, but they keep them hidden and rarely shared at work. Consciously or not, their answers influence their attitude, behaviour and their workplace productivity.

The answers will tell you what your employee wants, what they are missing, how they are feeling and why they behave the way they do. If you knew these answers, they would inform, even transform, your strategy and your business imperative to inspire each member of your team. The answers invite personal responsibility for taking positive action to create an environment where everyone brings all their talents to the workplace. That is when they reach for their full potential in their pursuit of your business goals and their personal expectations. This is when your life, and theirs, become more rewarding and more fulfilling. Definitely less frustrating, confusing and tiring! It's the win–win environment we all want to create at work.

Will this mean that you as their manager or team leader will soon be achieving greater business success? And with less stress?

Our promise is that your team will go above
and beyond what was once expected of them to
believe that this can become a reality. Imagine the
possibilities!

We do hope that you enjoy the quest!

Anna and Peter

How to Use This Book

It is not just about decoding a generation; it's about cultivating a collaborative environment where Gen Z can thrive. It is a work environment where they can contribute their unique perspectives and abilities and co-creating a workplace that is truly vibrant, inspiring and forward-thinking.

We provide you with the building blocks to actualise this vision, enabling higher self-motivation, engagement and exceptional performance as tangible outcomes. Each building block, based on one of the eight key questions, is significant and plays a vital part in creating an exciting and inspiring work culture.

As you navigate through the questions, you'll discover a variety of strategies designed to facilitate communication and drive progress. These tools are at your disposal. You can use them regularly and integrate them into how you communicate and interact with your team. Together with the building blocks, they will make all the difference in how you win with Gen Z, see Figure 0.1.

Whether you choose to explore the chapters sequentially or focus on specific areas of interest, each chapter is a valuable resource. Use them to adapt your strategies, try new approaches and experiment based on your unique situation and challenges. It will enable you to future-proof your business and cultivate a workplace that not only attracts but also retains top talent. We know that Gen Z will react positively and feel inspired by your collaborative approach.

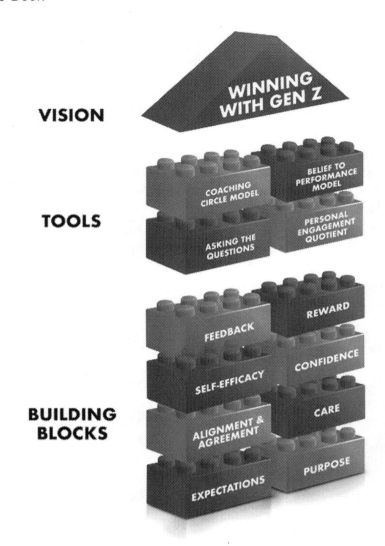

VISION

TOOLS

BUILDING
BLOCKS

FIGURE 0.1   Building with Gen Z.

Working with Gen Z: The Expectations, the Challenge and the Collaboration

1 CLOSING THE GAP

Through the eyes of some employers and in the media narratives, Gen Z is frequently portrayed as being entitled, having unrealistic expectations, being impatient and difficult to manage. They are seen as a generation that is reluctant to go the extra mile, prone to anxiety, has short attention spans, is easily distracted and readily offended.

Gen Z, when they arrive in the workplace, often notice a clash of expectations. They speak of uninspiring leadership, poor development opportunities and unmet expectations. There is a lack of continuous feedback and disagreements on work–life balance. They feel restricted in their creative entrepreneurial expression, undervalued and unfairly compensated. They notice instances of greenwashing, reduced commitments to environmental responsibility, or insufficient diversity, equity, inclusion and belonging (DEIB) initiatives, contrary to what the company's annual reports might suggest. About 44% of Gen Z feel that their employer does not understand their generation. Around 75% of them feel uncomfortable sharing a personal viewpoint due to fear of judgement or discrimination.[1] This survey highlights a significant gap in expectations and experiences between employers and Gen Z employees. However, it's a gap that can be closed.

When Gen Z employees join the workforce, their unmet expectations focus attention on vital elements of the work environment which may have been overlooked, ignored for review or accepted as "normal" in the past. If these expectations are not recognised, there is a risk that they will pack up and leave. Providing them with the necessary support and understanding, Gen Z can bring about substantial, positive changes in the way we all work.

Through collaboration, flexibility and communication, new possibilities and exciting aspirations can be imagined and achieved by everyone who is committed to winning at this game we call "work".

As a team leader, manager or business owner, how effectively does your business currently meet the needs, expectations and challenges of Gen Z? Being aware of these demands will help you stay relevant and competitive in today's fast moving work environment!

Here are some questions that you might consider. They begin to close the gap between what the best of Gen Z expects and what your business needs.

---

1 Randstad Holding UK (2024) www.randstad.com accessed 01-02-2024 available at www.randstad.com/workmonitor/

Alignment of personal values and company mission:

- *Do you understand the personal values and priorities of your Gen Z team members, and how well these align with the mission and purpose of your company?*

Feedback culture and high-performance environment:

- *How does your company incorporate Gen Z's desire for continuous and customised feedback into its commitment to fostering a high-performance environment?*

Awareness of strategy:

- *How much emphasis is invested in explaining the long-term strategic direction of the company and what this means for Gen Z and the role they will play in shaping the future?*

Learning environment for motivation:

- *In the pursuit of business tasks, how does your company's dedication to creating a learning environment contribute to maximising the motivation of Gen Z?*

Communication preferences:

- *How does your business currently communicate with its employees? Are you utilising the necessary tools and platforms to maximise the effective collaboration and communication that Gen Z is comfortable with?*

Contributions impacting company success:

- *How does your company ensure that Gen Z team members feel perpetually engaged, through knowing that their contributions have a meaningful impact on the success of the organisation?*

Tech-savvy generation and business benefits:

- *Where, when and how is Gen Z applying their tech skills to support your company and accelerate the business benefits of technology? How does your company's digitalisation strategy align with what Gen Z expects and the future business needs?*

Results-oriented priorities and inclusive collaboration:

- *How does your company's emphasis on results foster a culture of collaboration and inclusivity, valuing the diverse skills and experiences of individuals, in pursuit of business objectives?*

Work–life balance integration:

- *How does your company balance Gen Z's priority of seeking a personal work/life balance with the demands of business practices, ensuring it benefits everyone?*

Continuous monitoring of team well-being:

- *What strategies does your company have in place for monitoring and supporting the continuous health and well-being of every team member, including those from Gen Z?*

Career trajectory and advancement:

- *How do Gen Z team members recognise their own career trajectory and advancement within your company's overarching purpose?*

Recognising and nurturing entrepreneurial flair:

- *How does your company recognise and nurture the innate entrepreneurial flair of Gen Z to inspire motivation and discover innovative solutions to complex challenges?*

Describing a generation can be challenging.[2] It means making generalisations. However, there is a wealth of research and survey data available that sheds light on the typical characteristics of Gen Z and how they perceive their work environment. The "Gen Z and Millennial Survey"[3] conducted by Deloitte in late 2022 and early 2023 as well as Gallup's report "State of the global workforce 2023"[4] provide valuable insights into Gen Z's experience of, and mindset towards, the workplace.

With approximately two billion individuals globally in their cohort, Gen Z is a broad and diverse group born between the mid-1990s and early 2010s. They are becoming increasingly visible in today's workplace and by 2025 they are projected to make up nearly 30% of the global workforce.[5]

With their unique characteristics and values, Gen Z is likely to test traditional notions of leadership and management. By creating a work environment that supports the needs and aspirations of this generation, leaders can stimulate innovation, increase productivity and create a more inclusive and sustainable future. Gen Z has the potential to bring significant positive change to the workplace, and beyond!

2 UNDERSTANDING GEN Z

---

2 See Appendix II for a description of all generations from 1901 to today.

3 Deloitte Global (2024) deloitte.com accessed 01-10-2023 available at www.deloitte.com/global/en/issues/work/content/genzmillennialsurvey.html

4 GALLUP (2024) gallup.com accessed 01-10-2023 available at www.gallup.com/workplace/349484/state-of-the-global-workplace.aspx

5 Qureos (2024) qureos.com accessed 01-10-2023 available at www.qureos.com/hiring-guide/gen-z-statistics#top-generation-z-statistics-for-employers-in-2023

This generation is the most diverse, tech-savvy and entrepreneurial to date, and they have a strong desire to make a positive impact on society and their planet. Gen Z's digital fluency and ability to adapt quickly to change make them a valuable asset for organisations seeking to innovate and stay ahead of the curve. By embracing the strengths of this generation and adapting to their needs, organisations can attract and retain top talent, develop their potential and achieve long-term success, for them and the company.

Gen Z came of age in a world characterised by uncertainty, economic instability, mounting mental health awareness, political upheaval and growing concerns about climate change and the environment. On top of this, the prevalence of uncontrolled "addiction" to mobile phones and the constant search for approval on social media can lead to self-doubt and limited aspirations. About 46% of Gen Z indicate that social media affects their well-being negatively.[6] These circumstances, as well as the way they may have been parented, influence their perspectives and approaches to working in an ever-evolving job market.

Furthermore, the Covid-19 pandemic 2020/21 had a substantial impact on their lives, their happiness and their ability to nurture and maintain relationships. According to a study by The Workforce Institute[7] 51% of Gen Z participants felt that the remote learning and education system failed to prepare them for future work life. It also revealed that the struggle of remote learning led to challenges in developing

---

6   Deloitte (2023) Gen Z and Millennial survey 2023.
7   UKG Workforce Institute (2024) www.workforceinstitute.org accessed 01-10-2023 available at https://workforceinstitute.org/meet-gen-z-optimistic-and-anxious/

communication skills, which can be essential in the workplace, such as developing relationships, resolving conflict, confident negotiating, public speaking and networking. Until these challenges and skill gaps are addressed, they will persist, affecting their careers and their working lives.

Nurturing interpersonal relationships on a one-to-one basis, or realistically assessing their own ability to make an immediate impact, presents difficulties that may never have been addressed until they arrive at work! The responsibility for encouraging the practice and development of these skills is now becoming a necessary obligation of bosses, managers and team leaders.

3 WORKING WITH THEIR ASPIRATIONS

One notable outcome of these influences is that Gen Z is actively seeking roles that express a sense of purpose. They prioritise finding careers that align with their values and contribute to positive societal impact. However, alongside this desire for purpose, they also place great importance on financial security and stability. They recognise the necessity to secure their future in an unpredictable world and acknowledge the challenges of buying a first home and managing high living costs.

Sustainability and environmental consciousness are regarded as essential principles for this generation. They expect companies to fully embrace these priorities as they themselves aspire to them. Social issues like climate change, racial injustice, diversity and income inequality are at the forefront of their minds and they make decisions about where they want to work based on whether the company shares their values, or not. About 48% per cent say they wouldn't accept a job with an organisation whose values didn't align with theirs on social and environmental issues and on having a positive impact on the world.[8]

This generation is often referred to as "digital natives" since they were the first generation to be born into a completely digital world. Research suggests a pressing need for companies to accelerate their digital transformation to align with Gen Z and exploit the commercial opportunities of a fast changing world. Gen Z experiences frustration with outdated solutions, slow communication and illogical information sourcing.[9] They expect technology to be accessible and to help them do their work more efficiently and with better results.

Gen Z uses technology to gather information quickly and make informed decisions about their career choices. This generation looks for references and services offered by companies like *Glassdoor*[10] and *Great Place to Work*,[11] to support their decision-making process. They aren't afraid to move on if a job or company doesn't meet their expectations in terms of the role or work environment.

A survey conducted by the Project Management Institute in 2023 suggests more than 59% of young professionals in the United States are likely to leave their jobs solely because they are not satisfied with

---

8 Deloitte (2023) Gen Z and Millennial survey 2023.

9 London School of Economics and Political Science (2024) www.lse.ac.uk accessed 01-10-2023 available at www.lse.ac.uk/business/consulting/reports/empowering-generation-z-and-millenni als-to-deliver-change

10 Glassdoor LLC (2024) www.glassdoor.com accessed 01-10-2023.

11 Great Place to Work Institute (2024) www.greatplacetowork.com accessed 01-10-2023.

the sense of fulfilment they get from their work.[12] Two major factors were identified: a lack of opportunities for growth and learning, and the feeling that they are not making a meaningful contribution, for example, being involved in decision-making.

Another variable that is very important to Gen Z is where they do their work. About 65%[13] of Gen Z expressed their preference for a hybrid or remote work setup, and a significant number of Gen Z seek flexible working hours to allow them to raise families, care for family members and pursue hobbies and interests. This might prove to be a difficult balancing act whilst companies are trying to find their way in this new hybrid world.

One of the main reasons given for the preference towards hybrid/remote work is the strong desire for a healthy work–life balance. This aspiration is important for Gen Z individuals, and it stands as the foremost quality they admire in both their leaders and their peers. They do not consider high stress levels to be acknowledged as evidence of commitment, loyalty and hard work.[14]

4 STRESS AND BURNOUT

Worldwide, only 23% of employees under the age of 40 report feeling that they really care about their work.[15] Results from the Deloitte survey of 15,000 Gen Zers show that 46% of them feel stressed, anxious or even "burned out" at work all or most of

---

12 Project Management Institute (2024) www.pmi.org accessed 01-10-2023 available at https://community.pmi.org/blog-post/74493/the-state-of-the-american-worker#_=_
13 Gen Z and Millennial survey, Deloitte, 2023.
14 Deloitte (2023) Gen Z and Millennial survey 2023.
15 GALLUP (2023) *State of the Global Workplace: 2023 Report.*

the time due to the high intensity and the demands, as they see it, of their working environment and managers focused only on results.[16]

Deloitte's research found that Gen Z's experience of stress is due to a number of different factors. These include everyday financial struggles, the high cost of living, worries about their long-term financial stability, concerns about unemployment, constant connectivity and information overload and anxieties about the well-being of their families.

However, it's not solely personal worries that contribute to the stress levels of this generation. Other factors in the workplace play their part too. Excessive workloads, imbalance between work and personal life, unsupportive managers, unhealthy team dynamics and experiences of harassment and microaggressions. Just over six in ten Gen Z workers have experienced intimidating physical advances or physical contact, receiving deliberately offensive and inappropriate emails, undermining behaviour based on gender, vindictive and corrosive exclusion, and prejudiced jokes at work which are dismissed as banter.[17]

5 SUPPORT, FEEDBACK AND DEVELOPMENT OPPORTUNITIES

Gen Z are not only looking for companies who care about making an impact in their sphere of influence. They are also looking for employers who support their employees' personal development, training and career opportunities.

---

16 Deloitte (2023) Gen Z and Millennial survey 2023.
17 Deloitte (2023) Gen Z and Millennial survey 2023.

Gen Z grew up in a highly competitive and individualistic educational environment. They have become accustomed to instant feedback through online platforms and digital tools, such as learning management systems and educational apps. Their teachers were monitoring their progress and providing developmental feedback throughout their academic journey.

Gen Z now expects a similar level of responsiveness and accessibility within their professional workspace. The Workforce Institute survey showed that almost one-third of Gen Z is inclined to put in more effort and stay longer with a company when they have a manager who provides support. In contrast, 37% wouldn't tolerate an unsupportive manager and would consider leaving the job.[18] They seek a workplace characterised by psychological safety,[19] where they feel valued, can confidently challenge the status quo, are willing to take calculated risks and can admit mistakes without the fear of negative consequences.

The fact that Gen Z live in a world where feedback is readily available, from social media "likes" to online reviews, has created a gap between their expectations and how they might experience feedback in the workplace. Gen Z considers feedback at work crucial for their engagement and job satisfaction, and 43%[20] prefer receiving regular, real-time manager feedback rather than during a scheduled performance review

18 Meet Gen Z: Hopeful, Anxious, Hardworking and Searching for Inspiration, (2019). Workforce Institute.

19 Fortune Media (2023) www.fortune.com accessed 01-10-2023 available at www.fortune.com/well/2023/11/21/psychological-safety-gen-z-work-employee-burnout/

20 Meet Gen Z: Hopeful, Anxious, Hardworking and Searching for Inspiration, (2019). Workforce Institute.

once or twice a year. Without it, passion, energy and creativity start to die.

6 A PERFECT COLLABORATION?

If leaders can tap into this generational shift effectively and harness the unique strengths of Gen Z, there is the potential to enhance employee engagement and drive it to new heights. They will experience the acknowledged motivation of Gen Z, their independence, adaptability, their desire to learn and improve themselves, their social and societal awareness and their energy. Gen Z are looking for employers who recognise potential, emphasise learning and personal growth, promote team working, offer financial security and a healthy work–life balance — a perfect collaboration.

If you don't know where you are going…any route will get you there.

Rudyard Kipling

Question One

Do I Really Understand What Is Expected of Me...?

A Gallup study[1] shows that only one out of two employees has a clear understanding of what is expected of them at work. And if we study the question of expectations, on a deeper level, it is not quite as simple as it might seem. In this chapter, we'll explore the different aspects of expectations and how they can become clearer.

1.1 UNDERSTANDING EXPECTATIONS AT WORK

Knowing what is expected of us forms a cornerstone of employee engagement.[2] It provides clarity, direction and helps us prioritise and plan our workload. This is particularly crucial for Gen Z as lack of certainty can result in hesitation, loss of commitment, time-wasting and reduced resilience, especially when faced with challenging circumstances.[3]

---

1 Gallup (2023) *State of the Global Workplace: 2023 Report.*
2 www.gallup.com/workplace/285674/improve-employee-engagement-workplace.aspx
3 www.gallup.com/workplace/285674/improve-employee-engagement-workplace.aspx

DOI: 10.4324/9781003475613-1

In the role of a manager, there is a constant and ongoing conversation about expectations to be had with your team members. Helping your team to have greater clarity on goals and clarity on direction drives higher productivity and motivation. Research[4] even suggests that it will have an impact on whether your team members, or some of them, will show up for work or not! Is there a gap between their expectations and yours? Any gap may take both of you to close it up.

If you were to ask your employees if they knew what was expected of them at work, the initial reaction for most people would be "Yes, of course".

Try adding "Really?" Who do they need to ask to find out? Who needs them to make their own job possible? Who do they need to make their job possible? What expectations do they have of you, as their manager? When you start to ask these kinds of questions they will see there is more to it then they, and probably you, first realised.

The modern business landscape is changing rapidly. It's not just about new ways of working or new places to do the work; it's also influenced by a shift in customer and consumer priorities, new technology, economic constraints and political factors. In this dynamic environment, the role and function of teams are also changing.

1.2 CHANGING WORK ENVIRONMENT

Today, teams are often cross-functional, and team members are responsible for delivering results in different projects. By leveraging the strengths

---

4 www.gallup.com/workplace/285674/improve-employee-engagement-workplace.aspx

of individuals from various functions, cross-functional teams aim to break down silos, improve communication and enhance the overall efficiency and effectiveness of projects within the organisation.

This structure might be beneficial and often essential, but it could also end up being challenging, especially for someone who is new to the workforce. Team members may find themselves reporting to both their functional manager and their cross-functional team leader or peer. This dual reporting dynamic can create confusion and potential conflicts, as team members may need to balance competing priorities and expectations.

This dynamic doesn't necessarily pose a problem for Gen Z. If there is anything that they are used to, it is change. Change is a part of their life experience and this generation has no issues with ever-changing priorities.[5] However, they may need support in determining what the changing priorities of others may be and the reasons for them. They may need prompting to make sure that they are constantly aware of the expectations that others have of them. Without clear appreciation of what others need, whatever hard work or energy we apply, chaos or disappointment will follow.

1.3 THE CHALLENGE: KNOWING WHOSE EXPECTATION IT IS?

When working in a team, all members will have slightly different expectations of each other and there will be different expectations of what should be done, how and when it should be done and what will be achieved by doing it. For a Gen Z, who wants to do a good job, to contribute and make a positive impact, understanding

---

5 D. Stillman and J. Stillman (2017). *Gen Z @work: How the Next Generation Is Transforming the Workplace,* Harper Collins.

the expectations of others will be essential in establishing what is, in turn, expected of them.

Very often expectations are created, and constantly modified, in the heads of other people. This can be very annoying, but it happens all the same! Their expectations keep changing. This is why communication and transparency are vital and a Gen Z employee will be looking at you, as their manager, for support. Support may mean initiating the conversation, listening to and discussing what they believe is expected of them. You will have expectations too, and whilst these may take priority, Gen Z will want to recognise where the company's expectations provide a route for their own learning, growth and reward. Here are some questions that will start the conversation:

- *What would your team, your customer and your suppliers, internal and external, say if you asked them about their expectations of you?*
- *How long has it been since you last asked them? What might have changed?*
- *What would be the evidence that you understand exactly what is expected of you?*
- *How would you know, in one year, that you've done a good job?*

Taking ownership of what is expected of them is key. They will have contributed to creating it, discussing it, accepting it and recognising how these expectations can support their goals. They won't be able to say they didn't know, they didn't understand or to blame others for the results. Only now will they have a solid framework for taking on all the challenges of the role. You can trust that they will have a clear understanding of what is expected from them!

My name is Leona and I am three years into a promising career that I have thoroughly enjoyed! But, a recent promotion brought a different, and not entirely positive, set of challenges and I found myself stuck. Not just stuck, but completely overwhelmed, and a bit demoralised.

As a self- starter and someone who takes initiative, I have learned a lot since joining this company. I am always willing to change, adapt and work with various teams in different departments. My efforts and results have clearly been recognised and this recent promotion was significant, a big break. It promised an exciting future with the same company that had given me the opportunity as a graduate three years ago.

I soon realised that certain assumptions were made with my appointment. I had to determine my own way of working, including coordinating with a U.S. team in a different time zone. My role, what was expected of me and an understanding of the bigger picture that I was now a part of, were all a bit vague and not really agreed. Whilst my direct boss was quite happy to leave me to it, another director, whom I rarely saw, expected quick results.

This feeling of uncertainty has never been my style and I started asking myself if this was the time to look for a new challenge outside the company? I think my manager picked up on this because he was checking in fairly regularly.

I didn't want to move on and I realised that navigating this situation alone was far from ideal. I took the initiative to set up a meeting with my manager. We needed agreements on how I would work, what my boundaries and constraints were, what results were expected, and how I would be supported in this new territory. Perhaps getting to know each other better would help?

Our meeting changed everything. My manager asked me about my priorities, my personal goals for the job, my concerns and the support I would need from him. I felt he had confidence in me. We agreed that after learning more about my new area and what was expected of me I should draw up my own route-map highlighting goals and time-scales. We set up a date for our next meeting to review the plan, discuss progress so far and agree on some next steps. One important part of this plan was to share it with the other director to ensure she was aligned with my priorities.

Now, I felt like part of a team with my boss. The direction is clear, and expectations are agreed upon. I feel back in control.

Project Manager, Medical Tech Industry

Gen Z wants to contribute and to make an impact. This is also in alignment with what is generally expected from every member of a business team. Imagine a sports team where once the players are on the field, there is only one leader, the coach who is not playing. Sometimes there is a vital role to be played during the game, to take a lead in a tactical move where the coach is not on the spot and cannot immediately direct. Occasional small leadership interactions with the acceptance of teammates can make an immediate difference.

When you, as a manager, encourage them to take initiatives you'll empower your Gen Z employee to be proactive and take charge of their responsibilities and sometimes take the lead. It's a way to support them to feel more in control and confident in their role and it can also lead to more autonomous decision-making, which is highly valued by this generation.

Reflecting on your own business strategies, what expectations do you have of your team members when it comes to them being both a player and a leader? Where might similar interventions be the "right" thing to do? How might your team make a valuable contribution to results? And most importantly, are they aware of this expectation?

Here are some questions that will help Gen Z to put themselves in control of expectations and for you, as their manager, to provide feedback and input to make sure it complements the bigger picture and what you are wanting them to achieve:

- *Where do you expect to be on this project by, say, the end of the month?*

1.4 WHEN EVERYONE IS BOTH A PLAYER AND A LEADER

1.5 ASKING QUESTIONS TO CONFIRM UNDERSTANDING

- *What is your plan for supporting the team's goals?*
- *What could prevent you from delivering the results you promised?*
- *What are your customers and colleagues expecting to achieve from your activity?*
- *Exactly how may I support you?*
- *What do you want to do first to move this forward?*
- *What do you want to focus on once you've achieved the first objective?*

These kinds of effective questions achieve two immediate results. They put a frame around any subsequent action and make success much more likely to follow. Effective questions raise the level of awareness in the performer's mind about the issue being explored. These questions also invite responsibility for owning their goals, recognising the potential obstacles, formulating a plan and making an agreement to deliver what is expected of them, and on time!

1.6 LIVING THE VALUES OF THE ORGANISATION

Expectations in the workplace are not only made up by the deliverables that need to be met or the service that your customers expect but also embedded in the values of the organisation. Most businesses have their own set of values, written or merely understood. They are the principles and beliefs that provide a cohesive vision and define how you are meant to work as a business. These values, when respected and reflected, influence, even dictate, the behaviours that are expected. For Gen Z, who are highly value driven, it is essential to see an alignment of values and behaviour and it is also important that they feel connected to the company values on a personal level.

Does everyone in your team know what the organisation's values are? Everyone should know them, agree with them and make decisions referenced to them. It will be an imperative context when it comes to creating an understanding of what is expected of everyone in the workplace, regardless of role and responsibilities.

However much you publish them, discuss them or learn them by heart, the values of your team and organisation are recognised and judged only by the behaviours and attitudes which are noticed in every interaction. Think of the companies and businesses that have impressed you. You will have experienced their values in action. Their values are what their reputations are built upon.

Gen Z will be attuned, even more than previous generations, to noticing values. They know that they will be expected to demonstrate the values of the company in whatever they do. By asking these questions you'll help your team uncover another layer of what is expected of them:

- *What behaviours are you noticing in the organisation, team, department?*
- *What value is being expressed from what you notice?*
- *Is that what we want to express? If so, how is it linked to our company values and strategy? If not, what behaviours would you like to be observing and experiencing?*

Sometimes there is a misalignment between what we say we value and represent and the behaviour that we choose. In order to support all team members in understanding and practising the company values, open up discussion with questions like:

- *What does it look like when we're demonstrating the value of, say, integrity and ethics, respect, innovation, drive, trust, etc. [insert your own values] in our company/team?*
- *How do we support each other to practise our values and how do we speak up when company/ team decisions and behaviours aren't in line?*
- *How do we communicate our values to our customers, both verbally and through actions?*
- *What part do our values play in our recruitment and promotion decisions?*

By having these discussions, one to one, or in a team meeting, and valuing each person for reflecting these values, everyone, especially Gen Z, will know without doubt what's expected of them.

1.7 AND FINALLY, SOME MORE QUESTIONS FOR YOU TO ASK YOURSELF...

- *Do you know what is expected of you in your role as a manager or a team leader? On a score of one to ten? Identify what would be different if the score was higher. What actions would make a difference to how you rate yourself? Verify expectations with customers, other departments, your own boss and your team.*
- *What aspects of your leadership and support, your work approach, and the service you provide, are important to your team?*
- *Does your team really know what's expected of them?*

You've got the tools. You've got the questions.
You only have to ask! Do they understand what is expected of them? Really?

The next question everyone is asking themselves, but
the leader rarely hears is...

"Do I know why it is expected of me...?"

This is the true joy of life, like being used for a purpose recognised by yourself as a mighty one.

George Bernard Shaw

Question Two

Do I Know Why It Is Expected of Me…?

Gen Z are often recognised for having a strong desire for doing meaningful work, and they seek employment with organisations that align with their personal values and beliefs. This is one of the reasons why it's so important for this generation to understand the organisation's mission, purpose, values and objectives. It helps them to feel they belong. The potential alignment can boost motivation and engagement. This is the arena which delivers high performance.

2.1 HIERARCHY OF NEEDS AND HOW TO FEEL FULFILLED

Maslow's Hierarchy of Needs[1] identifies that alongside our basic living requirements and safety, we are looking for three other needs to be met:

• The need to feel a sense of belonging and being valued by others.

1 World of Work Project (2023) https://worldofwork.io/2019/02/maslows-hierarchy-of-needs/ accessed 01-10-2023 available at https://worldofwork.io/2019/02/maslows-hierarchy-of-needs/

DOI: 10.4324/9781003475613-2

- The need to be recognised and acknowledged for our contributions and to value ourselves for being whoever we are.
- The need to realise and achieve our potential and to find purpose and meaning in our lives. Maslow calls this "self-actualisation" and it is considered to be one of the main contributors to motivation.

When people know only *what* is expected of them, the highest need that they can meet would be the recognition and acknowledgment of others. When people know *why* it is expected of them, things change!

Now they are invited to have a view of the final objective. They can see and experience in their imagination the fulfilment of the creative journey. They are part of an exciting process. They can utilise their strengths and skills, add their own ideas and make their own unique contributions. And for independent thinkers, like Gen Z, who like to be involved in decision-making, this will help them to feel acknowledged by others and most likely help them to create a feeling of meaningful belonging.

There is a connection between wanting to learn and grow, and self-actualisation. Continuous learning and personal development are key components of the journey. Gen Z places a high value on this as it supports them in getting ever closer to the amazing person they have the potential to become.

When they are aware of the bigger picture and how their strengths and expertise fill an important gap, they will be a resource for feedback, creativity and energy. They may offer suggestions for changes that can be considered for improving their own team's service. They are now contributing, and they, with others, can see the value they are bringing.

The most powerful benefit a manager can provide to employees is to place them in roles that allow them to apply the best of their natural selves, their talents, their skills and their knowledge, every day.

Gallup 2023

2.2 THE POWER OF A CLEAR PURPOSE

A company's purpose is the "why" behind a company's existence beyond simply making a profit. It is the unique reason the company has been founded or continues to operate successfully. It may be written down but should certainly be discussed with, and known by, everyone. It gives an insight into a company's culture that can be recognised and valued by all employees and customers, internal and external. It tells you why they do what they do. It's about promoting how their offerings and the manner in which they are delivered to the market differentiate them from other suppliers.

A company's purpose frames the work of employees too. Here it is about something larger than job roles and business results. Being clear on purpose is essential in defining what is expected of every member of the team and why. The aim is to unite everyone's efforts and energy.

Connecting our day-to-day work with the purpose of the company can have a profound impact as it serves as a guiding force that aligns individual tasks with the broader mission. Employees find motivation and engagement in understanding how their contributions fit into the larger picture, fostering a sense of pride and commitment. However, it is an important piece that is often overlooked and this is highlighted in a Gallup study where more than 3,000 workers, across different industries, were asked about brand identity. The study shows that only 41% of employees strongly agree with the statement "I know what my company stands for and what makes our brands different from our competitors".[2]

Here are some examples of the stated purpose of a company, from various industries, that shape every transaction for both customers and employees:

Hilton Hotels: ...*to fill the earth with the light and warmth of hospitality by delivering exceptional experiences ... .every hotel, every guest, every time.*

Ebay: ...*to empower people and create economic opportunity for all.*

Tesla: ...*to accelerate the world's transition to sustainable energy.*

Bank of America: ...*to help make financial lives better through the power of every connection.*

Nike: ...*to bring inspiration and innovation to every athlete in the world. And if you have a body, you are an athlete.*

Facebook: ...*to give people the power to build community and bring the world closer together.*

These company purpose statements encapsulate the essence of their missions, reflecting a commitment to making a positive impact on the

2 GALLUP (2024) accessed 01-10-2023 available at https://news.gallup.com/businessjournal/156197/employees-don-brand.aspx

world. Teams and team members who are a part of an organisation that is working with a clear, living purpose know every day what's expected of them and why. They will be more inspired, better equipped to prioritise tasks, to make decisions and manage their time more effectively.

Today, there are still some leaders who may dismiss the question of purpose with the notion that "they don't need to know." There is a pay-off for them in taking this position. They think it's quicker, easier and saves time. However, if Gen Z or any other employees are left without this context in which to work, there can be a significant cost to the organisation in terms of decreased engagement, lack of performance and problems with retention.

To ensure that the company's purpose genuinely resonates with employees and has a significant impact, they will need to be aware of it. If there is not a widely recognised and publicised purpose statement, or if it is too vague to have a significant impact, ask your team to create their own purpose.

2.3 OWNING AND COMMUNICATING THE ORGANISATION'S PURPOSE

Beyond business tasks, targets and goals, how would they describe their purpose? What is the greater good, the improvement and the benefit they bring to the company that would be recognised by everyone and every team they serve, and to the wider community? An example might be: "We are committed, through innovation and collaboration, to equip project managers with precise, timely, and insightful data, to empower informed decision-making and project success." Then support everyone to promote it!

Questions to ask your team:

- *What is our organisation's purpose and objectives and what are the team's purpose and objectives?*
- *How does our purpose relate to the goals we've all agreed and the numbers we're keeping an eye on?*
- *How would others recognise what differentiates our team, our organisation, our products and services?*
- *What makes our company unique on an emotional level? What does each member of the team think and feel? Are they inspired?*
- *What would we be doing if we had the reputation of being the best team in our industry?*
- *How can I, as a part of the team, support the team to turn our purpose from words into actions and behaviours?*

2.4 KNOWING HOW THEIR ROLE FITS IN

Go to any meeting of department heads and area managers and you are likely to hear a lot of input from each as to what is going on in their area of responsibility. They assume that their boss, who has called the meeting, is responsible for the bigger picture. They are paid to look after their own patch and that is where most of their interest lies. They will make decisions to optimise only their interests without aligning it to the overall strategy. So the chances are that for them the big picture extends only to include what they need to report upwards to the boss.

Operating in silos like this can lead to significant problems such as communication barriers, disastrous decision-making and internal conflict. This approach may contribute to missed business opportunities, difficulties in resource allocation, inconsistencies in the customer experience and ineffective problem-solving. Moreover, it could foster a sense of disconnect for employees if they perceive their roles in isolation.

The "why" of each person's role is knowing how their contribution matches the purpose and objectives of the company, and makes a difference. Gen Z will be quick to identify where their role contributes to the whole purpose and mission of the company and how it is valued by everyone. They want to see how their efforts become a part of the whole service that is finally delivered to their clients and customers. This is why Gen Zs look to be invited into customer facing meetings, even if it is merely to observe.

My name is Alison and I'm a senior leader and board member in the logistics industry. We run a Graduate and Apprentice Programme for our new recruits. The aim is to train, develop and, we hope, retain the talent who have joined us. We are aware, especially with Gen Z, that they too are looking for a work environment that will meet their demands. They want to have their potential recognised, to be challenged, supported and to feel that what they are doing has a meaningful purpose both for them and the company.

We had some important projects which were designed to explore possibilities for improving our services and researching new markets. But business got in the way and we didn't have the resources to prioritise them.

Here was an opportunity, I thought, to delegate these projects to the participants of the programme. A lunch meeting was set up for all of the 'grads' and apprentices to connect with each other and more importantly, to meet and get to know some of the senior leaders of the business. Participants were offered a well-defined brief, clear expectations and a deadline of three months to deliver their proposals. We promised that every successful project delivery would launch their initiatives into the business.

The senior leadership team stepped into a coaching role, guiding and supporting the teams throughout the process. As the delivery day approached another lunch meeting was set up for the presentations of solutions. They had demonstrated analytical skills and a future-focused mindset in presenting not only clever but practical, innovative, solutions. Two projects were set to launch immediately while the remaining two would follow in six months.

Our company is showing immediate benefits from these projects. This collaboration of traditional experience and youthful creativity is now embedded in all our programmes and personal development plans.

We want everyone who joins us in the future to find an inspiring home for their energy and latent talent. We know that Gen Z will have a lot to contribute to our future success.

Board Member, Logistics Industry

2.5 GEN Z BRINGS A DIFFERENCE

This generation is acutely aware and accepting of diversity, and they place value on every connection that enhances the effectiveness of their role, regardless of its source. Companies which focus on the benefits that different perspectives, backgrounds and preferences bring to the table recognise obvious commercial advantages and gain respect from Gen Z. When companies embrace diversity in their working practices, they are promoting a wider range of perspectives that will add more energy, viewpoints and challenge in order to maximise the value of discussions and decisions.

Like everyone else, Gen Z brings a difference too. That unique difference is the reason why what is expected of them is so important to the organisation. Here are some questions to discuss with your team:

- *What makes each of our team members unique in their job and where do they add value (both knowledge and financially) to our organisation?*

- *How is our commitment to diversity benefiting our company's bottom line?*
- *How and where is each person's contribution and perspective acknowledged and appreciated?*
- *How does valuing DEIB express the company's purpose and lead to more job satisfaction as everyone understands not only what is expected of them but why?*

Typically, we view customers as external entities or organisations with whom we engage to sell our goods and services. But, in fact, our "customers" are all around us, including internally within the company. We spend our entire day serving our "customers" in the workplace and being served by them. These "customers" are our colleagues, internal teams, our boss and our employees.

Consider the finance department in this context. You supply them with information about your project and request specific data or a specific service based on that information. In this case, you are the "customer" and the finance department will be the "supplier". Making sure your requests are clear and giving all the needed details help the finance department understand what you need so that they can deliver the right kind of service.

Discovering what an external customer really wants so that you too can exceed their expectations requires some element of sales skills. To be competitive and one step ahead, everyone in a sales role might ask their customers:

- *What are your key frustrations in dealing with people like us, or products or services like ours?*

2.6 WHAT DOES YOUR "CUSTOMER" REALLY WANT?

If your company consistently seeks feedback from customers to identify these frustrations and commits to overcoming them, they gain insights into what the customer really wants and why, enabling them to supply it.

The same principle works inside your organisation too.

Remember, your colleagues are also "customers", inside their own departments and across the organisation. How are your Gen Z team members serving their colleagues? How are your Gen Z members being served?

Ask other departments what frustrations, however small, they have dealing with yours. Find out and work together to make improvements. This is the main reason behind any kind of work that we do – to make a difference, to make things better, easier, more satisfying, more purposeful and ultimately more rewarding.

When, together, you work out and supply all these missing pieces, those gaps in your service that the "customer" accepts as normal but secretly wishes could be a little bit better, everyone will have triumphed.

That's why Gen Z and all the team members do what they are expected to do. It really matters to someone.

2.7 FINALLY, SOME MORE QUESTIONS TO ASK YOURSELF...

- *Do you understand WHY you are doing what's expected of you as a manager? On a scale of one to ten, how effectively does your day to day work connect to the bigger picture and the company's purpose?*

- *Identify what would be different if the score was higher. What actions could you take that would make a difference?*
- *How can you support your team members to connect their roles to the organisation's vision and purpose?*
- *What can you do to keep drawing out the big picture and challenge everyone to bring fresh views to every meeting?*

The next question that everyone is asking themselves, but the leader rarely hears is....

"Do I agree...?"

The two most important days of your life are the day you were born and the day you find out why.

Mark Twain

Question Three

Do I Agree...?

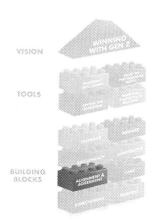

Gen Z, unlike many generations before them, are looking at the workplace as just one arena, where they can strive, take on challenges, learn, grow, be valued and achieve a potential that is already within them and that they are longing to express. Until they are aligned with what's expected of them, and why, they will rarely contribute their best performance and they will struggle to find a level of co-operation that will integrate them with the organisation. Without this alignment there will be a diminution of commitment, passion, energy and engagement.

Do you think they agree with what's expected of them? For them it's a job. It pays the bills. They may also want to impress, to develop their skills and earn more money. They may have other aims too that do not always align with the aims of the organisation. Achieving the business tasks and goals may serve merely to provide for their basic needs. Perhaps their passion, their energy and their sense of self-worth and well-being are complemented by activities outside the workplace. They may be absorbed by hobbies,

DOI: 10.4324/9781003475613-3

sports, charity work, family, exciting new experiences, learning new things and many more.

When what they are expected to do at work matches and complements what they feel is really important and meaningful to who they truly are, only then are they getting fully "on board", willing to contribute maximum energy and resourcefulness.

3.1 AGREEMENT BEFORE INITIAL RECRUITMENT

Before recruitment is the easiest time to discuss and assess agreements of what is expected of each other. Gen Z will want to know the values of the organisation and what they feel the company can do for them. Before they join the organisation you will want to be confident that they know they have a role in which they can offer what you are looking for.

Beyond the customary discussions, before recruitment decisions are made, there are questions you could ask to get a feel of what's important to them and what values drive their ambition. They are equally relevant to your present colleagues too.

- *Where have you experienced feelings of pride at work?*
- *When have you felt that your work is more meaningful to you than at other times?*
- *Where have you recognised a match between our company's purpose and mission and what you think is important in your life?*
- *When in your life, either at work or elsewhere, have you failed to achieve what you wanted, disappointed yourself and accepted that another succeeded where you did not?*
- *What did you learn from these events and how did you change your approach to the next similar situation?*

- *How do you think that what's expected of you will bring greater benefits to both you and to the organisation?*
- *What support could we offer that would make you feel confident to maximise your energies, initiative and creativity in pursuing and achieving the objectives of our organisation?*

Gen Z is likely to be as selective as you to ensure that the organisation they are considering joining will offer them a framework that provides for their needs and matches their values. When both parties agree there will be immediate accord from the start that will set the tone for what will hopefully be a long lasting and profitable relationship.

Be prepared for them to ask you:

- *What are your organisation's values and purpose (though they should have done some research!)?*
- *In practice how do you expect these to be demonstrated in your daily interactions with colleagues and customers?*
- *Is there a difference between how colleagues are treated and the attitude shown to customers?*
- *What are examples of the career trajectories of colleagues in your organisation and what support did they receive in achieving their success?*
- *How will I know how I am getting on so that I can maximise my experience and learning?*
- *What are your protocols for meeting the work–life balance aspirations of everyone in the organisation?*
- *Whom may I speak to, in a similar role, who can tell me a little more about what it's like working here, from their perspective?*

Agreement of what's expected at the beginning is the best possible introduction to an effective business relationship. However, the initial induction period is crucial. During this time, employees evaluate how well the company is fulfilling its promises. This is why it's important to set clear and realistic career progression plans instead of overpromising.

3.2 WHERE IS THE MEANING?

Gen Z also look for meaning in their work beyond making their pay cheque and providing the material needs for themselves and their family. Perhaps the meaning for them lies in what they are learning? Perhaps in the satisfaction of serving others? Perhaps in having responsibility for coaching and developing teams? Or it could lie in the ultimate difference that their contribution is making to a bigger goal, far beyond their job.

For some, if not many, their sense of meaning could be the thought that whatever their role, that eventually their product or service must, at the end of the line, bring satisfaction, security, happiness, health, excitement, contentment or delight to people who they may never know. What they have been a part of, will, for someone in the world, if only briefly, have made it a better place.

THE SEARCH FOR MEANING

"The greatest task for any person is to find meaning in his or her life." These are the words of Viktor Frankl whose book "Man's Search for Meaning[1]" describes the terrible conditions he endured in Auschwitz concentration

1 Frankl, V.E. (1962). *Man's Search for Meaning: An Introduction to Logotherapy,* Beacon Press.

camp from 1942 to the end of the war. He was a young psychiatrist and upon entering the camp, and being assigned to work duties, he committed himself to surviving. He decided that his promise to himself was eventually to join family members who were living in Canada, and to continue his contribution to the world as a psychiatrist.

He noticed that of those few who survived all had an intense desire to achieve a goal or complete some unfinished project after the war. They had their meaning, a clear purpose. Most of the small number, spared as labour, who might have had the possibility to survive, did not. They had surrendered themselves to an inevitable fate beyond their control. For them there was no meaning. Viktor was determined to use his time in captivity, and his professional skills, to study the entire experience; how it impacted on everyone, the prisoners and their guards.

Each day his existence had deep meaning. He survived, went to Canada and wrote up his observations in his best-selling book. He continued to make a meaningful difference for the rest of his life.

3.3 GETTING INTO THE "FLOW STATE"

When we engage in a task that holds personal meaning, which presents a suitable challenge without overwhelming us, has a clear and achievable goal and allows for focused concentration free from distractions, we begin to meet some of the criteria necessary to experience a "Flow State".[2] The concept of a "Flow State" was introduced by Mihaly Csikszentmihalyi, a Hungarian psychologist renowned for his work on motivation, happiness, and positive psychology.

In this state, we are immersed in an activity that makes us neither anxious (if it's too hard) nor bored (if it's too easy). When a performer, whether in sport,

2 Csikszentmihalyi, M. (1998). *Finding Flow: The Psychology of Engagement with Everyday Life,* Ingram Publisher Services.

work, or art, finds themselves in this state, they excel in their performance and often lose track of time because they become fully absorbed in what they're doing. They always report how great it makes them feel.

Being in a "Flow State" is similar to being "in the zone". It is also experienced by some as a state of relaxed concentration. Most of us have experienced it, if not always at work, certainly in other areas of our life. There is no distraction through tension or tightness, merely an extreme awareness of what is happening in the "now". There is absolute clarity on the end goal whilst accepting total responsibility for achieving it.

Does your Gen Z team feel trusted enough to establish necessary boundaries to facilitate this state of effective concentration? Do they feel supported to cultivate a sense of independence and autonomy in which they are more likely to experience this state while working?

- *To what degree do they feel the task has meaning for them?*
- *Are the goals for the task crystal clear?*
- *Is the task appropriately challenging?*
- *What measures are in place to minimise interference?*
- *To what degree is there freedom as to how the task should be delivered?*

There is no guaranteed route to a "Flow State" but it's magic when you find it.

> *Working for something we don't care about is called stress. Working for something we love is called passion.*
>
> **Simon Sinek**

3.4 HOW DO YOU KNOW IF THEY AGREE, REALLY AGREE?

At first, just ask! "How do you feel about this task/assignment/role?" Do they feel excited, exhilarated, confident, supported and energised? Or do they feel anxious, intimidated, uninterested or resistant?

It's a question of feelings. How they feel about agreeing with what's expected of them will be reflected in how you yourself feel. Their answers to questions, their contributions to discussions and their body language will give you the clues.

The challenge for the leader is to pick up on these clues. When you know how they feel, you will have identified a potential gap between a merely adequate performance and the possibility of an amazing one. You may have to dig a little after their initial reply:

- *On a scale of one to ten, if ten is your highest sense of agreeing with what's expected of you, where do you rate how you feel right now?*
- *If your score was one number higher what would be different?*

Naturally, they will feel compelled to imagine a new scenario. Their reply will bring out, into the open, what has not yet been expressed. It may not be the full story but now you have a starting point for respectful discussions. There may be learning by both parties as you listen to each other and explore what is getting in the way of complete agreement. With greater understanding, there may be a pathway to close the gap completely and reassess the score to a ten!

The next question that everyone is asking themselves, but the leader rarely hears is....

"Who cares...?"

In my experience there are two great motivators in life. One is fear. The other is love.

If you manage people by love – that is if you show them respect and trust – they start to perform up to their real capabilities. They can take risks. They can even make mistakes. Nothing can hurt.

Jan Carlson
Ex President and CEO of SAS Group

Question Four

Who Cares...?

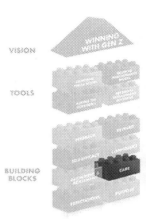

Gen Z, the future of your workforce, with their abundant potential, skills and energy, thrive in a corporate environment that acknowledges and values their needs and ambitions. They are asking "Who cares?" and they need to know that what they do matters to someone.

When they feel that they know who cares, their commitment to personal and professional growth is turbo-charged. If they don't know, then the enthusiasm they brought with them will dissolve. They may stay and do enough just to get by but more likely they will leave and look for another job elsewhere.[1]

The generations who came before Gen Z arrived at the workplace as new employees with little expectation that anyone would, at first, actually care very much about them or their well-being. They would find a structure, teams to work with, tasks to accomplish, goals to achieve, bosses to report to, occasional

1 GALLUP (2023) *State of the Global Workplace: 2023 Report.*

DOI: 10.4324/9781003475613-4

reviews to measure work results and rewards dependent on the company's perception of you and your progress. There was a ladder for the ambitious to climb. When the going got tough, the attitude was to not make a fuss or ask for help but to try again.

Is that your experience? Imagine an organisation where no one cares for anyone other than themselves and their own work responsibilities. Of course, it wouldn't work. It wouldn't even get off the ground. The correlation between the knowledge that someone cares and the energy and passion brought to the workplace is precise. Gen Z knows this from their learning experiences growing up. They will be expecting similar support at work.

Knowing who cares is one of the many things that Gen Z says are important to them.[2] Where previous generations learned to repress and not express, with Gen Z it's the other way around. Having an insight into other things that Gen Z are likely to care about invites the possibility of opening up conversations with everyone in the team. When you listen closely, you'll begin to address their question of "who cares?"

4.1 WHAT MATTERS TO GEN Z?

A proactive approach not only elevates team morale but also contributes to a workplace culture where employees feel valued, supported and motivated. You will be tapping into a new and vital resource that may still be laying frustratingly dormant. Here are some questions that you can ask your team that show that you prioritise the care of your team members:

2 *Meet Gen Z: Hopeful, Anxious, Hardworking and Searching for Inspiration* (2019). Workforce Institute.

- *What activities do you enjoy outside the workplace? Would you appreciate time off instead of bonuses or pay for overtime as recognition for exceptional results?*
- *How well do we notice others' feelings, and do we pick up clues that could lead to constructive and positive discussions?*
- *In what instances does displaying kindness boost engagement, while the presence of intolerance serves as a demotivator?*
- *Are we ready to set aside biases, and values that might lead to disagreement and discord by influencing workplace decisions?*
- *Are we aware of the impact of mental wellbeing within the company? E.g. is there an appreciation of the difference between "being anxious" which is commonplace and "anxiety" which can be a debilitating condition?*
- *With new ways of working, which may lead to more solitary work, is there active encouragement for value-adding face-to-face meetings and team gatherings?*

Promoting discussions, and action follow-up, on these questions will be a powerful influence on answering Gen Z's question "Who cares?"

An old man was walking along the beach near his home in California early one morning. In the distance he spotted a young man performing what looked like an exercise routine. As he got nearer he realised that he was stooping down to pick up something off the beach. He would take a few steps towards the sea and, with a huge sweep of his arm, throw it into the ocean. He went up to the young man and asked "What are you doing?" He replied "The starfish have been left stranded by the outgoing tide. If I don't throw them back into the sea they will die."

> The old man said *"Don't you know that there are thousands of starfish all over the beach, and this beach goes on for many miles. You couldn't possibly make a difference".*
>
> The young man merely stooped down and picked up another starfish and threw it back into the ocean. *"I made a difference to that one!"* he said.
>
> The old man realised the wisdom of the young man's words and changed his plans for that day. He joined the young man and together they spent the morning throwing starfish into the ocean.

Here are instances that might seem like standard business practices but actually underscore the absence of the caring culture you aim to foster:

4.2 WHEN I DON'T CARE

1. Emails sent to everybody on the list to "cover my back" rather than to meet people's need to be informed.
2. Managers setting goals that their direct reports feel obliged to accept whilst doubtful that they will successfully deliver them.
3. Managers switching priorities for their teams without sharing the bigger picture or cancelling meetings at the last minute without explanation.
4. Innovations or new creative ideas suggested by team members not being valued for consideration or acknowledgement as a sincere contribution to potential improvements.
5. Not offering to support a colleague before they are in a position of having to ask for it, if indeed they do.
6. Taking a telephone call that cuts across an important conversation a manager is having with a team member.

7. Managers who pick up on every mistake, shortfall or problem whilst ignoring evidence of positive activity and commitment.
8. Managers who micromanage and insist on being included in every decision, however trivial.
9. Appraisals where the "brownie points" are given only for the increased productivity and none for having courage, taking risks and being committed to innovate and change.
10. Managers, who have arranged for colleagues to attend training courses, but fail to brief them beforehand or support the application of what they learned after they return from the course.

And these are just a few examples! These instances, often dismissed as standard business practices, reveal a potential shortfall in cultivating the caring culture we aspire to instil.

Recognising and addressing these subtle yet impactful aspects will contribute to fostering a culture where care, understanding and collaboration thrive.

4.3 WHERE IS THE "CARE" IN YOUR MEETINGS?

The one place to start emphasising a commitment to building a caring environment is in your meetings. Some even say that the way meetings are run reflects the way the company is run. How true is this for you? If you call or attend a meeting, how do you convey that you value everyone for attending and that they all feel valued?

- *Do you declare your purpose for the meeting and get agreement at the beginning?*
- *Do you ask everyone for their "intended outcome", what they want from their time spent*

in the meeting both for themselves and for the organisation, and do you share yours?

- *Do you invite members to switch off their phones, email notifications, and laptops (when appropriate) or ideally leave them outside the room to allow participants to be fully present and actively participate?*
- *Do you make sure that all participants, including Gen Z, have a voice in the meeting?*
- *Do you check on a time schedule that suits everyone and stick to it even if the entire agenda is not completed?*
- *At the end of the meeting do you ask whether "intended outcomes" have been achieved?*
- *To improve the quality of future meetings, do you ask: "What worked?" "What could have worked better?" And apply the learning at future meetings?*

In every "event" there is an opportunity for learning and improving and to make things better. Showing your caring side takes no more time and the rewards are infinite. A caring atmosphere is characterised by a sense of safety, allowing individuals the freedom to experiment, challenge, share information and support others.

My name is Haydar and I'd been with the company for about five years when I was asked to take on a leadership role and become a manager. The company was re-structuring, merging two departments in our division into one. That meant that a well-liked team leader was to be made redundant, and I was to have responsibility for the new, enlarged department.

There would be exciting new prospects for the company, improving processes, expanding services and opening new centres. However, I faced a challenge as two recent Gen Z employees expressed concerns about the impact on their jobs, current responsibilities, and future expectations. I felt they were not convinced. If they had concerns, so did I. What if we couldn't work effectively together? What if I couldn't do this new job? What if the team didn't like me?

Realising that we needed to function as a cohesive team from the outset, I decided to have one-on-one conversations with each team member. I wanted to understand their expectations, how they saw their career development, what interested them most about their job and how they saw the company's values aligning with their own priorities. I tried to encourage an open discussion about any doubts or fears and inviting suggestions on how we could progress together.

I got to know them better and learned a lot. I was listening to them, and they felt they were being heard. I noticed more enthusiasm for building our new team collaboratively. Ideas were shared not only from existing members but also from the recent recruits. We explored and agreed upon new roles and discussed how we could offer support to each other when needed. My role became clearer too!

With everyone now on board I felt more confident that we could now focus together on working towards our business goals.

Manager, Parts division, Consumer Products Importer

4.4 YOUR CARE ACCOUNT …. KEEP IT IN CREDIT!

Creating a caring environment really makes a difference to how a work culture is experienced, especially for Gen Z, who rank it among the top three most important leadership qualities.[3]

There is no need to check every behaviour to analyse whether it is caring or not! Instead, think of it like your CARE ACCOUNT with others, as if it was an account in a bank. When you're in credit, where you have a reputation for caring for your team, occasional

---

3 *Meet Gen Z: Hopeful, Anxious, Hardworking and Searching for Inspiration* (2019). Workforce Institute.

withdrawals, like forgetting an agreement, giving a brusque instruction, making a negative observation, etc., aren't a big deal. We're all human! And there are so many possible lapses!

Here's a typical example of the response you might get depending upon the credit in your CARE ACCOUNT. Imagine you are in a team meeting, and you ask for brainstorming ideas. When someone puts forward a suggestion and you reject it with "We tried that two years ago, before you joined this team, and it didn't work". You then ask "Has anyone got any better ideas to offer?"

If your CARE ACCOUNT is low, or in debit, what happens? It all goes quiet, and to get any more ideas up on the white board will be like getting blood out of a stone!

However, what would be the result if you had a healthy credit in your CARE ACCOUNT? Your team member might smile, make a joke of it and then offer some other ideas.

Being aware of the balance in your CARE ACCOUNT will ensure the likelihood of a positive response. Demonstrating care should be a constant, not something you turn on and off.

It is essential to find out where more care is needed. It's in these areas where efforts are wasted, disenchantment begins and motivation ends. To find out, you've just got to ask your team.

4.5 CARING MEANS BETTER RESULTS!

The question is simple "How much do you enjoy yourself in your work?" A ten out of ten would indicate fulfilment. A number below three is a cry for help! Gen Z will let you know straight away if you are caring enough, provided they feel comfortable expressing it. If not, they'll tell you in your annual EOS[4] results. A score out of ten itself isn't necessarily precise except that it leads to the next question:

- *Imagine that you are now in the future and that your score is just one point higher. What is now happening that wasn't happening before that makes you feel that work is a little bit more enjoyable?*

Asking the questions in this way invites the team member to take responsibility for both the awareness of where they currently are on their original score and their picture of where they would prefer to be. In other words, to describe what's missing. For example, here are some you might hear:

- clearer direction
- better communication
- more efficiency
- more enthusiasm
- better meetings
- more inclusiveness
- better planning
- better time management
- more responsibility
- more feedback

These observations shine a spotlight on where more care could deliver better outcomes. At this

4 Employee Opinion Survey.

point the discussions might move uselessly towards blaming others. "If only other people would change then I would be happier". Is this a definition of powerlessness? To help bring them back into a feeling of control and knowing that someone does care, ask:

- *What might be a first step, however small, that you could take to move towards the situation that you would really like?*

It might be as small as talking to somebody else who does care, and together supporting each other to have something happen, and to take action.

It will be effective if you, as their manager, encourage them to take that first step. For two important reasons – the double-win. Firstly, a move towards more enjoyment or satisfaction is usually a move towards extra productivity and greater profits. Secondly, taking the action pro-actively puts them in control of changing circumstances and delivers a powerful private message – "I am worth it!"

When you focus on the question "Who cares?" it will be known to everyone that at least one person does care. You!

The next question that everyone is asking themselves, but the leader rarely hears is...

"But can I do it...?"

Dreams are extremely important. You can't do it unless you imagine it.

George Lucas

Question Five

But Can I Do It...?

VISION

TOOLS

BUILDING
BLOCKS

Most people will ask themselves "Can I do it?" when presented with a new challenge or a difficult job. Gen Z may appear confident but could be anxious and reluctant to admit it. To provide effective support or challenge, first understand their true feelings.

The feeling of being able to create for real the very ideas and projects pictured in our imagination is known as "self-efficacy". Promoting self-efficacy is of paramount importance in building an organisation, a team or each one of us. Self-efficacy plays a significant role in shaping one's motivation, performance, and overall career success.

What is Gen Z likely to be thinking as they discuss what is expected of them with you? Are they creating mental images of themselves, either doing the task really well, struggling to get it done or even, not doing it at all?

Acknowledging these mental images and thoughts will be really helpful because they represent your team member's belief in their ability to succeed, to get the job done and to feel good about it. If they genuinely

DOI: 10.4324/9781003475613-5

think they will manage to do it, that will create positive energy which will help them as they take on the task.

If they can't picture themselves succeeding, how will that influence their attitude? Will it turn defensive, timid, fearful or even angry? Will they feel anxious knowing they've made a promise to deliver? Listen out for the word "try" as in "I will try and do it". "Try" is a conflation of two attitudes, "I intend to do it but I think I may not be able to". Their doubt will tell you the outcome is likely to disappoint. To understand what they are thinking and feeling, look for changes in their behaviours and attitude towards the task at hand.

Questions to ask yourself:

- *Do they look for excuses to explain a failure to deliver what is expected of them?*
- *Do they detach themselves from their agreed responsibility to carry out the task effectively?*
- *Do they identify and consider alternative choices of action or procrastinate and end up doing nothing?*
- *Do they look for someone else to do it for them?*
- *Do they go quiet and into their shell?*
- *Are they reluctant to take an initial step that may not be part of a previously accepted process for fear it won't work or be approved.*

Their attitude and potential lack of self-belief could hinder progress unnecessarily both for the team and for themselves. It will lower any certainty of them accepting a similar challenge in the future. Thus the need for regular check-ins and feedback.

In encouraging their positive attitude, belief in themselves and the likelihood of a successful outcome, consider asking yourself the following questions before assigning the task:

- *Do they have access to the necessary resources and support to accomplish the task successfully?*
- *If the task is a new challenge for them, is there a back-up plan in place to support their intention in the event of a loss of direction or an unforeseen obstacle?*
- *Has the task, and their role in achieving a successful outcome, been discussed and agreed by the individual, the team and me as the manager?*
- *Have I involved them in the task assignment process, allowing them to express any preferences or concerns?*
- *What support, if any, will they need?*
- *When will they deliver what they promise? Is this agreed?*
- *What learning do they want to achieve from this new experience?*

5.1 CHALLENGING BELIEFS

Different beliefs and attitudes lead to different behaviours. The river of energy flows from belief at its source to the performance at its mouth.

Belief → Attitude → Behaviour → Skill → Performance

The impact of beliefs and attitude on someone's performance is significant. How we behave and the quality of our performance are directly influenced by what we believe is possible and how we approach things. The attitude of an employee or a whole team can often be detected when they are presented with a challenge … their body language, facial expression, signs of hesitancy or enthusiasm give clues about their own private belief, whether empowering or limiting. It gives you a sense of whether they feel confident in taking on the specific task assigned to them.

Table 5.1 shows how the energy flows and leads to different behaviours based on the original belief. The beliefs, attitude and behaviours form the foundations of skill and performance, ultimately shaping both the quality and the result.

TABLE 5.1

The Interplay of Beliefs, Attitude, and Behaviour

Self-identification	Belief	Attitude	Behaviour
Victim	• There is nothing I can do about it • I have no choice • I'm not adding value	• Helplessness • Overwhelm • Worry • I give up	• Lack of action or decision making • Lack of engagement • Low self-esteem • Focus on problems • Avoidance • Take things personally
Aggressor	• For me to win, you need to lose • I'm right, you're wrong • I know better than you	• Resentment • It's all about winning • People are incompetent • Entitlement	• Lack of trust • Blame others • Controlling and bossy • Getting things done through force
Learner	• Everything is a valuable experience • Things happen for a reason – what can I learn from this?	• Curious • Open Minded • Motivated by learning	• Asking questions • Feeling motivated • Solution focused • Opportunistic
Co-creator	• There are no problems, only opportunities • We both win or we don't play • I need you and you need me	• We'll achieve more if we work together • Everyone is contributing • Positivity	• Autonomy and teamwork • Entrepreneurial • Inviting other's perspectives and knowledge • Looking for win/win

Source: Adapted from "Above or Below the Line", Conscious Leadership Group, LLC (2023). www.conscious.is, accessed 01-10-2023, available at www.conscious.is/video/locating-yourself-a-key-to-conscious-leadership

Where do most managers try to fix a problem? Either at the behaviour level "You seem unengaged, I want to see more commitment" or at the skill level "I want you to improve your presentation skills".

There is a different approach. Start at the belief level, to uncover why energy, passion and creativity might be low and where it's being spent? Our limiting beliefs often disrupt and distract us from success. They prevent us from taking on a challenge and stretching ourselves. When we become aware of the beliefs and thoughts we hold, we can question them and explore whether they are true and helpful, or not. Only when we raise our level of awareness about how our thoughts and beliefs are affecting us will we be able to start to address the behaviours, the necessary skills and the performance.

Questions you can ask your team members when you think there may be a negative belief or thought holding them back:

- *What are you thinking and believing about yourself and about this situation, expectation or challenge? Is this true and helpful?*
- *If there is a negative and limiting belief what would have to be different, and in your control, for you to believe that you can do this?*
- *What would be a first step that you could take that would be in your control?*
- *What is a positive learning from past events that you can apply this time?*

By asking these questions you'll challenge their perspective and open them up to other, more empowering, ways of thinking.

5.2 STARTING AT THE WRONG END

5.3 INFLUENCING SELF-EFFICACY

What makes your company unique and efficient are the processes that everyone follows, which make things work and produce the business results. Everyone knows that there is a process that enables them to do their job. If anything goes wrong, without a known process it would be difficult to identify the cause and instead we start to question our ability.

5.3.1 FOCUS ON PROCESS

Without a repeatable and practised process your team and team members may well be regularly asking themselves "Can I really do this?"

Any doubt or concern that is in the mind of a team member will be limiting their total commitment. Clarity on the process they are about to embark on, with a clear structure of support, is more likely to lead to an "I can do this!" response.

When reviewing a performance, focus on the double-win, the improvement of process and the continual development of individual capabilities.

- *What did you notice about the process?*
- *What worked for you, where could it have worked better? Are there changes that might be considered?*
- *What have you learned about the process and about yourself?*
- *What will you do differently in the next similar situation?*
- *What do we all agree is our process for each task, our team's way of doing it, the process that will produce the results that we are here to deliver?*

A process that is known and accepted as a standard practice and can be relied upon is the best platform for producing the results you want and the improvements that can always be made.

A manager who can recognise a team member's talents and strengths, and guides them to understand the positive impact these strengths bring to their daily tasks, gains substantial benefits for both the individual and the team.[1] Do you know your team member's unique strengths? Find out by asking:

5.3.2 PLAY TO STRENGTH

- *What skills or abilities do you believe set you apart and contribute significantly to the team's success?*
- *When faced with challenges, what strengths do you rely on to navigate and overcome them successfully?*
- *Are there specific tasks or projects where you feel you bring a unique perspective or skill set that others might not have?*
- *Reflecting on positive feedback you've received, what strengths or qualities are frequently highlighted?*

If your team member feels they can't do what is expected of them, there might be some gaps in knowledge or experience that need to be filled in. Maybe they simply lack a skill for which they may need some training. Can they learn what they need from colleagues? Is there any best practice from other departments that your team members can tap into? Is an external training resource more suitable? Learning and development are essential for Gen Z. The more overt and agreed the better!

5.3.3 TRAINING AND DEVELOPMENT

---

1 Gallup (2024) accessed 01-10-2023 available at www.gallup.com/workplace/505523/powerful-duo-strengths-engagement.aspx

As you move to source the training requirement and make the arrangements, there are some key strategies to employ that most managers know, and only some follow.

- *Agree with the team member what it is they want to learn on a course or workshop, or from a colleague, and where they will apply their new knowledge and with what beneficial effect – ideally in bottom-line terms.*
- *Review the key learning points after the course and agree to a plan whereby the team member uses the new knowledge on purpose and with regular supportive reviews and feedback from you as their manager.*
- *A final review after six months to assess progress and competence – and to put a bottom-line value on the difference that using the new skill is making.*

5.3.4 WHEN THE PROBLEM SEEMS TO BE OUTSIDE THEIR CONTROL

Sometimes we point the finger at an obstacle and say "I can't do it and this is the reason why…"

- Time
- Priorities
- Clash of interests
- Insufficient resources
- It's not the company way, etc.

If solving the problem is part of the team member's responsibilities which are already agreed, and progress seems out of their control, the discussion might need to shift towards exploring alternative courses of action:

- *What options do you have to overcome these obstacles that you haven't yet tried?*
- *What will you do first and what support do you need?*

Taking an action, however modest, as a first step whenever things seem out of our control, is at the heart of developing our creativity and ability to persuade and convince others when the route ahead appears blocked.

But what if it's not external obstacles but rather internal doubts that might be getting in the way? Each time someone insists, "It can't be done," it reinforces a sense of powerlessness. Instead, we want to foster feelings of control and empowerment. And how do you accomplish that? Here are some questions you could use when dealing with a team member who is hesitant to take action due to the belief of "I can't":

- *What is the picture you can imagine, once the obstacle is no longer in the way, that shows you are one step closer to your goal?*
- *What would have to be different to enable this thing you want to happen, to actually happen?*
- *Which of these things/events/people can you begin to influence? What difference would that make?*
- *Which do you want to choose first to take action on in order to move towards your goal?*
- *When will you do that and what support, if any, do you need?*
- *When can we catch up and review where you are and how you are getting on?*

5.3.5 TEAM SPIRIT AND COLLABORATION

When you ask "To what degree do you feel what's expected of you?", you may well get a less than enthusiastic reply. But what if you asked a different question? For example, "To what degree do you feel **we** can do what's expected of **us**?" Asking the question about **us** will relax the pressure on the individual and begin to develop trust, mutual respect and interdependence. This is now team talk. Sport shows us perfect examples of teams solving challenges together.

These are some questions that will start the process of believing "yes, we can do it." Then it's a short step to believing "yes, I can do it!"

- *Can we do what is expected of us?*
- *What obstacles or problems might we encounter?*
- *What can we do differently to close the gap or gain an advantage?*
- *What do we see as our individual roles in overcoming an obstacle?*
- *What do we need to do in order to carry out our roles effectively?*
- *How have we confirmed what it is that others in the team are relying on us to deliver?*

THIS IS A TEAM. THEY COMPETED IN THE SEOUL OLYMPICS IN 1988

David Whitaker was the hockey coach who inspired the team to win England's first gold medal for an Olympic team event for forty years. England were drawn against Pakistan in the Olympic semi-finals, a team which was ranked above the England squad. Pakistan had a powerful weapon in their armoury. They had the reputation of rarely losing the ball in a tackle – they would win nine out of ten. Imagine if David had asked team members "How do you feel about your ability in tackles against Pakistan?" He would have had some not very encouraging replies.

Instead, he asked the team "What can we do together to meet this challenge?" and together the team created a tactical plan. They each agreed to take responsibility to ensure that they passed the ball before being tackled, hugely changing the odds away from Pakistan. They agreed a strategy that offered an instant 'support squad' for any of their teammates who were in possession of the ball. The moment a Pakistan player approached to tackle, the ball was passed. The game was taken away from them, literally, and England won through to the finals, and eventual gold.

When the strategy was devised and practised and perfected what would the answer be to David's question "Can we do that?". "Of course we can!" ... and they did!

Discussions about how to approach challenges as a team like this emphasise that each participant is part of a system and that no part is dispensable nor greater than the whole. This is a team working in harmony, knowing that together they will find the ability they need to do whatever a task demands. Teams and individuals will always ask themselves "Can I do it"? The difference now is knowing that there is a way!

Whenever you hear an "I can't" there is an opportunity to help someone to build their self-efficacy.

It's worth pursuing every time!

The next question that everyone is asking themselves, but the leader rarely hears is...

"But am I confident...?"

Life begins at the edge of your comfort zone.

Neale Donald Walsch

Question Six

Am I Confident in Doing What's Expected of Me...?

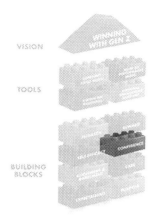

Have you ever considered the impact your leadership has on the growth of healthy confidence and self-belief among Gen Z team members? They may not point the finger at you and say you are the cause of their potential lack of confidence, but you are the best placed person in the team to influence them and to keep their performances up to the highest standards that their potential offers.

Gen Z team members want to move forward in their working life, they want to see progress and they want to have clear steps to reach their goals. However, if they're held back by low confidence, they'll need you to guide them on their path and help them to find their next stepping stone to the future of their choice. This is what they are used to from their years at school. Consciously or not, they will expect the same from you.

DOI: 10.4324/9781003475613-6

In this chapter we'll explore the enormous positive impact you can have on their work environment. It may mean reflecting on your own management style and seeking out, together with your employee, how they see a future for themselves and the initial steps they are willing to take from where they are now, to where they want to be. It starts with asking them the question:

- *How confident are you feeling, doing what is expected of you?*

6.1 THE IMPACT OF STRESS ON OUR CONFIDENCE

Moving forward means having the confidence to try something new. They may be holding themselves back. They may avoid attempting new things and learning from new experiences. In every aspect of all our lives there is a level of activity beyond which we may hesitate to go. Avoiding negative stress, the stress that hinders performance, is a strong motivator. Conversely, positive stress, the stress that can raise levels of adrenaline, is a benefit that contributes to exceptional high levels of performance. Actors, public speakers, athletes, those in the workplace and many other performers, know what this means. It's no different for Gen Z!

Taking a step beyond what feels normal and comfortable is taking a risk. It's new, it feels strange, it looks like it is going to be resistible. However, this is precisely where learning, growth and confidence can be discovered. This is where they will realise more of their potential, develop their abilities and add real value to your company. Whether or not they take that step and keep progressing may depend largely on your support and encouragement.

Having feelings of stress is a part of the human condition and we all experience stress in our lives. It is not stress itself that is the "enemy"; it is our reaction to it that causes any problems.

The stress that holds us back, the anxiety, the tension and feelings of reluctance in the workplace are often the result of feeling you are in a place where you don't want to be, unsure of what you are doing and why, doing things you don't believe you can do or things you don't want to do. And no one supporting you or caring enough to help you make any positive change.

Whilst earlier generations may accept that these experiences are all part of the job, Gen Z have different expectations. Their life experience so far tells them that it need not be that way. They look for customised structure, identifiable learning steps and exciting goals within their reach. They want the confidence to take on greater challenges and be valued for it.

6.2 REFRAMING NEGATIVE THOUGHTS

Our thoughts and feelings generate our reactions to our circumstances. For some, these are positive and energising and individuals cultivate a mindset focused on optimism, belief in their abilities and a sense of empowerment. Such a thought often leads to a feeling of enhanced motivation, resilience and creativity. For others, their thoughts and feelings are negative and limiting. They sabotage the willingness to take on new challenges, to learn and to grow. This is when the inner critic in our head, which judges and has an opinion about our every thought and every activity, begins to try and influence our actions.

If we listen to it and pay attention, we lose our focus. Trying to please the critic is a game you will never win! It takes away our awareness of what is happening, how we are responding and the ultimate goal we want to achieve. It is more helpful to reframe our thoughts to something more empowering.

Let the interference of the inner critic fade into the background whilst your inner observer takes your attention. The inner observer is always present in the moment; it never judges or gives advice but notices everything you need to be aware of in order for you to make the most appropriate and timely decisions. Empowering thoughts and awareness are vital and necessary elements for creating exceptional performance.

6.2.1 INTERNALLY

- *What is happening, what am I noticing most, what is my intention, what is really true?*

For some, sadly, the easiest way to feel better is to get out of the situation that they blame for causing how they feel. They will resist the challenge, or they will just leave and walk away. You will have lost a valuable asset who has much to contribute to your company.

Here are a few typical examples of where negative thinking interferes with performance:

- Worrying about the consequences of their decisions
- Regretting past events
- Blaming themselves or others for their present predicament
- Getting angry

- Trying too hard, getting tense and upsetting self and others

Which can lead to:

- Making careless mistakes
- Breaking agreements
- Procrastinating
- Lower self-esteem

As a manager or team leader, posing straightforward questions can help reframe their negative and stressful thoughts with more manageable and helpful ones, which will keep them present and in the moment. For example:

- *How are you feeling right now about your performance in your role?*

6.2.2 EXTERNALLY

- *What are you noticing most that is giving you this feeling?*
- *What if you could change that thought or feeling, what would it be like? What would be happening?*
- *When you doubt your abilities, what evidence supports those doubts? What evidence contradicts them?*
- *With a changed perspective of the current situation, what would that mean to you, where could that take you?*
- *What steps could you take to move forward? What would you choose, however small, to be the first step?*
- *What support would you want from colleagues or me?*
- *When can we meet to review progress?*

These questions are the pathway for the leader to start rebuilding confidence. The route for you as guide and supporter is to:

1. Listen!
2. Highlight just one observation of concern.
3. Invite a positive picture to replace the old negative one. Ask for more detail to lock in the affirmative and enticing possibility.
4. Encouraging the first practical steps which, with support, will distract from the negative view of their experience, and build confidence for early success, step by step.

My name is Shani. One of my team, Jayden, a young guy in his twenties was ready to take more of a customer-facing role in some of our projects. He was expected to keep close to customers, respond to immediate needs and to be aware of future business opportunities.

Although he was confident in his technical skills, engaging personally with customers left him feeling uneasy. Recognising his discomfort, I wanted to support and encourage him in his new role. With guidance, I knew there was an opportunity for growth.

To reverse the negative picture he was remembering from his recent experiences I invited him to picture a perfect meeting where everything had gone well, where he felt he had developed a closer relationship with the customer. I coaxed more detail from him until I too could see the positive picture that he was describing.

I asked him what measure would tell him how successful a meeting had been if he had to score it out of ten. One measure, he volunteered, would be to know everything we need to know about each customer.

I invited him to use the next meeting purely for finding out more about the customer and reporting back to the team. I didn't need to prompt him. He realised that the questions he could ask included current satisfaction levels, concerns and frustrations, future aspirations for the business, and likely challenges to be overcome in the future.

My questions to him had shifted his perspective on his role in these meetings. Jayden changed from worrying about a lack of confidence to wanting to understand more about the customer. He felt he could do that. Also, he knew he had support from me.

We meet regularly and I ask him about what worked for him in his recent meetings and what he felt might work better. He is widening his purpose to include more aspects of his role as his customers feel more confident in dealing with him.

I realised that all I had done was, by asking questions, to redirect his focus, enabling his natural, confident self-image to emerge. Clearly it is the little steps outside your comfort zone which, with support, will lead to the big transition. It was a win-win for both of us.

Senior Software Engineer, Tech Company

6.3 THE THREE CONSCIOUS ZONES OF ACTIVITY AT WORK

Figure 6.1 shows the three zones of experience which we all negotiate at times and which dictate our effectiveness in the workplace. You, your employees and Gen Z will always find themselves in one of them!

The purpose that underpins and motivates continuous and never-ending improvement, for your teams and your company, is to always be aware of the endless possibilities that expanding the perimeters of these inner circles can achieve (Figure 6.1).

The Comfort Zone represents the arena in which day-to-day practices feel normal. Pushing the boundaries of the Comfort Zone into the Learning Zone invites discoveries, the learning of new skills and expanded confidence. Growth and development follow and, of course, enjoyment. The Panic Zone will still be there which may be entered occasionally either with intent or by mistake but always with caution!

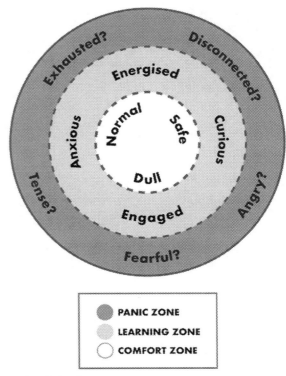

FIGURE 6.1 The Circle of Zones.

Sources: Adapted from L. Vygotsky (1978) and Tom Senninger (2000); Mind Tools Limited (2024) www.mindtools.com accessed 01-10-2023 available at www.mindtools.com/a0bop9z/the-learning-zone-model

6.3.1 THE COMFORT ZONE

In the Comfort Zone, individuals can be confident and know and value who they are and what they bring. Here is where they do things well, where they feel comfortable, where they feel safe, where they say to themselves about a situation or an activity, "That's normal for me, I can do that". Organisations that spend most of their operation in this zone are seen to be offering consistency to their customers and employees. They will say to themselves "this is normal for us, this is who we are". However, the downside of staying in a constant state of "comfort" can be individual boredom, frustration, doing tasks that others could perform more economically, loss of ambition and finally loss of loyalty. For organisations, it could eventually lead to loss of staff and loss of customers.

This is where most change takes place. Change may be imperative because of feedback that emphasises a need for improvement. It may be a necessary response to new circumstances, or it may be as a result of personal or company ambition, or a commitment to being the best that it is possible to be. Managers and team leaders, responsible for people, will encourage and support activities within the Learning Zone, recognising their significance for both individual well-being and the daily operations of the organisation.

6.3.2 THE LEARNING ZONE

Considering that Gen Z team members highly value learning and development opportunities, they expect to be challenged. In fact, learning and development opportunities are number two on the list of things that are valued the most when they choose an organisation to work for.[1] A McKinsey study reveals that 74% of Gen Z individuals cite insufficient development opportunities as a key reason for thinking about leaving their current job.[2]

However, the Learning Zone is not a place to stay for long. It's there to serve you, to encourage and support change. Beware that if your team members are permanently operating in a Learning Zone, it will likely lead to burn out. Continuous challenges can have a negative effect on overall performance.

---

1 Deloitte (2023) Gen Z and Millennial survey 2023.
2 McKinsey (2022) www.mckinsey.com accessed 01-10-2023 available at www.mckinsey.com/~/media/mckinsey/email/genz/2023/01/2023-01-17b.html

Job satisfaction may be affected if the demands consistently exceed capabilities. The risk of making mistakes increases with cognitive overload, jeopardising the quality of work and outcomes.

To mitigate these risks, it's crucial to balance Learning Zone activities with periods of rest, recovery and ongoing support. Regular assessments of well-being and workload management can ensure a sustainable approach to personal and professional growth. If not, the law of diminishing returns will apply. It may even lead your team member to the Panic Zone where little of continuing value is ever achieved.

6.3.3 THE PANIC ZONE

Here the performer is out of their depth and knows it! The rational solution is to review the situation and make some new decisions. The tenacious, high-risk tendency is to carry on regardless until other forces intervene to prevent any continued activity and damage. Many bosses are guilty of promoting the Panic Zone, or ignoring it when their team members are in it. They may have the best of intentions. They may believe there is no other option. But it's the perception of the person finding themselves in that position that counts. The boss may be blissfully unaware whilst any blame for inconsistent performance is levelled at the performer.

6.4 WHICH ZONE IS YOUR TEAM MEMBER IN?

You can get a good idea simply by asking them, "How confident are you feeling, doing what you are doing?" Their reply and their manner will give you clues. If you are in doubt, dig a little deeper until you are confident that you understand their true feelings. Which of their tasks mean they operate from their Comfort Zone? Is it the majority of their work? If it is, then you may want to challenge them and give them something that will stretch them and help them grow.

When you notice a drop in performance, or incongruent behaviour, their thoughts are likely to be unfocused and elsewhere. They could be bored and feel unappreciated in a Comfort Zone which is no longer comfortable. Or they could be feeling under pressure in the Learning Zone without any support, encouragement and no expectation of appropriate reward.

Whatever you notice, you may not know what is going on for them internally. It's not that their value and potential as an employee has diminished. They may merely feel that they are in the "wrong" zone.

Encouraging them to confront their frustration and inviting them to describe a new and happier situation that they can imagine and picture will distract them away from being fixated on negative self-limiting thoughts. Now, when invited to consider options for change, with support, they are in a more positive place to choose to take steps, however modest, towards a better situation. Then they will start to regain control.

Your decisions on where and when to delegate, and how a support network can be established, depend upon where in the Circle of Zones you perceive your team member to be. Their progress, learning and enjoyment are optimised on the edge of the Comfort Zone, just inside the Learning Zone. Too far and thoughts of survival block the learning. When staying safely in the Comfort Zone there will be little progress. Gradually moving into the Learning Zone is where their first steps towards change are certain to happen. Soon they will recognise that where they are operating has become closer to the new "normal" for them. This is confidence re-discovered whilst they

6.5 HELP THEM EXPAND THEIR COMFORT ZONE

now apply themselves to the necessary tasks and functions of their role.

When there is a new challenge, when you are reviewing progress, when you want to develop another's self-confidence, focus at first near the edge. With your encouragement, here is the start of a new journey. The impossible becomes the possible which, in turn, becomes the new "normal". Their confidence has returned! Here are some questions you can use to involve them in the process:

- *Is there a particular area in the team or company that you're curious to explore or learn more about?*
- *Are there training programmes or workshops you believe would be beneficial for your career development?*
- *What gaps, if any, have you noticed in your experience, knowledge or skill set?*
- *In what ways can I support you in stepping outside your Comfort Zone and taking on new challenges?*

With confidence regained, the next question that everyone asks themselves, but the leader rarely hears, is...

"Do I really know how I am getting on...?"

Tell me, and I forget, teach me, and I may remember, involve me and I will learn.

Benjamin Franklin

Question Seven

How Am I Getting On...?

Most Gen Z team members are looking to learn, progress and make an impact in your workplace and beyond. Feedback tells them if they are "on course" to their objectives and when and where corrections to the course need to be made. When the intention is clear and progress is ongoing, Gen Z values frequent feedback.

If your Gen Z team members are unaware of how they are performing, they may become disoriented. They will have little idea where they stand in relation to their goals, nor will they know what their next steps should be. They will either start making unfounded assumptions, guessing until it becomes apparent that they are struggling or they will turn to you for guidance, essentially transferring responsibility for their performance back to you as their leader.

Not knowing how they are getting on can have significant negative consequences for employees and their organisations. It can lead to disengagement

DOI: 10.4324/9781003475613-7

and a lack of investment in their work, resulting in decreased productivity and job satisfaction.[1] As a result, Gen Z, who expect clear, actionable feedback on their performance, are likely to put a lot of pressure on themselves and their performance which can easily lead to anxiety, frustration and resignation.

By engaging with your Gen Z employees and discussing how they are getting on and how they themselves perceive their progress, you can help them gain a clearer understanding of their strengths and areas of development. So often the company culture assumes that the responsibility of feedback rests primarily on you as the leader. When team members themselves assume this responsibility they have more clarity and appreciation on where they are on the journey towards their personal aims and business objectives. Providing employees with frameworks for learning and growth is a key driver of engagement. Employees who acknowledge that they have opportunities to learn and grow are almost three times more likely to be engaged in their work.[2]

When Gen Z knows with some certainty where they are in their development and NOT where they think they are, or want to be, they will be in the ideal place from which meaningful action and progress can continue.

7.1 APPRECIATION VS RECOGNITION

Recognition is the positive feedback from self and others based on performance or achieved results. It is also acknowledging the efforts and accomplishments of individuals and teams. Appreciation, however,

---

1 Gallup (2023) *State of the Global Workplace: 2023 Report.*
2 Gallup (2023) *State of the Global Workplace: 2023 Report.*

goes beyond performance and results. It's about celebrating and valuing individuals for who they are and the inherent potential they bring to the table. From a Gen Z perspective, both recognition and appreciation are essential components in building sustainable and healthy confidence. Combining these two forms of feedback nurtures the growth and well-being of Gen Z individuals in the workplace.

Although recognition can be highly motivating and exciting, it has limitations. It is performance-based, subjective, conditional and refers mainly to the past. Recognition may be scarce, and it can be stressful when many people are competing for a limited amount of praise. Appreciation, on the other hand, is unconditional and doesn't require performance or results. It can be as simple as listening, showing compassion, saying "Thank you", "Well done" or telling people what you really value about them.

7.2 MAKING FEEDBACK TRULY VALUABLE

To create a meaningful feedback conversation, one needs to move beyond quick judgments or generic comments such as "You did so well!" or "That's terrible!" Instead, it is vital that Gen Z performers become aware of specific information about what worked or didn't work. Traditionally, the manager does this by giving their observations about the employee's behaviour, attitude and performance, and how that impacts results and perceptions. However, doing it this way leaves out an important piece.

Sustainable and truly effective feedback can only be achieved when we also encourage the employee to reflect on their own performance. This type of feedback helps them take ownership of their performance and develop self-awareness, which is critical for constant never-ending improvement. As a leader, you can facilitate this by asking open questions such as:

- *Ideally, what were you intending to achieve?*
- *How did you feel about that performance?*
- *What did you notice about it?*
- *What did you learn from it?*
- *If you were able to do it again, what would you do differently?*

Here Gen Z is compelled to describe their goal or intention and reflect in detail their own performance accepting that effective changes start with themselves.

Another crucial aspect of making feedback effective is to align it with personal and organisational goals, values and purpose. Managers can enhance the impact of feedback and its relevance by inviting them to recognise the meaning and reasons why they have chosen to work towards their goals.

When feedback is tailored to an individual's specific strengths and chosen areas of improvement, they are more likely to become more motivated to change. Feedback, when aligned with the values and purpose of the organisation, can also help build a strong sense of belonging and shared purpose among team members.

While many of us understand the frameworks and reasons for generating feedback, putting it into practice can be challenging! Lack of time, fear of how their feedback will be received or not knowing

7.3 WHEN GOOD INTENTIONS RESULT IN NEGATIVE OUTCOMES

how to start an effective and actionable feedback conversation may hold some leaders back.

A research study[3] shows that nearly 45% of managers find giving developmental feedback difficult and stressful, with over 20% actively avoiding it altogether. Furthermore, 37% of the leaders represented in this study choose not to give their team members positive recognition.

It's easy for a leader to think they're maintaining good relationships and keeping their direct reports safe when they don't give developmental feedback, but in fact they're missing opportunities to unlock potential, address issues and ultimately make their own and their employee's lives easier.

Research shows that developmental feedback and the opportunity to reflect on one's progress are rare.[4] It is rare because managers avoid doing it and employees have stopped asking for it. Using a coaching circle model is a straightforward and time efficient way to start addressing this gap and to empower your team to take ownership of their development and to tap into their full potential.

---

3 Excel Communications Limited (2023) www.excel-communications.com accessed 01-10-2023 available at www.excel-communications.com/blog/6-uncomfortable-reasons-managers-avoid-giving-feedback

4 Gallup (2023) *State of the Global Workplace: 2023 Report.*

My name is Marcella. The performance at one of my branches, normally amongst the highest, was beginning to deliver below expectations. I needed to understand what was happening and to try and get everyone back on track.

The new manager, Josh, was popular with his team at first. He was supportive and encouraging. He was convinced that if he was too obsessed with results and too critical of anyone who was falling short of expectations, it would hurt morale and damage his relationship with the team. Instead, Josh thought that constant and uncritical praise would get the best results and would ensure he remained a popular leader.

However, the team was not learning and was no longer motivated. And it was getting worse.

I invited him to discuss how he conducted his reviews, how he generated feedback and what follow up actions were promised to embed any changes. He admitted that he rarely reviewed the performance of his team, and when he did, he was never critical and did not invite alternative and helpful actions to develop skills and effectiveness.

The very situation that he set out to avoid was happening. He was becoming less popular and less respected.

I suggested that he sit in on other managers' performance reviews, to learn from leaders who were excellent at generating feedback. I promised to support him as he made changes to his own reviews. I pointed out that these can be as frequent as he felt appropriate, weekly, monthly or just when the moment felt right.

The team responded well to clearer direction, took responsibility for making changes in their performance and felt valued by Josh for the improvements and the results they were achieving.

Area Manager, National Real Estate Agents

7.4 A COACHING CIRCLE

Coaching circles are designed to offer a structure for both a formal and an informal conversation and need not only be reserved for use as a tool in an annual performance review. The value comes from using it as a guide, often and regularly with employees, so that you and your team can leverage learning and insights. Gen Z, with their expectation of continuous

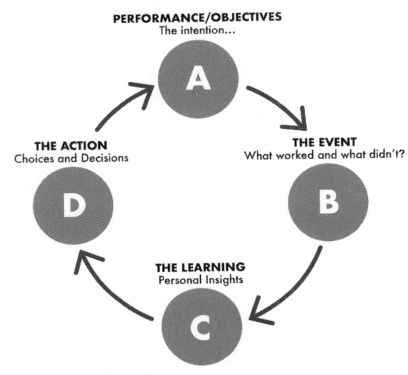

PERFORMANCE/OBJECTIVES
The intention...

A

THE EVENT
What worked and what didn't?

B

THE ACTION
Choices and Decisions

D

THE LEARNING
Personal Insights

C

FIGURE 7.1 A coaching circle.

development and feedback, will genuinely appreciate your commitment to it!

The Purpose: Follow the process of a coaching circle (Figure 7.1) to generate as much feedback as possible about a past or current performance. The performer can now identify and commit to an action that either leads to a goal or to modifying a previous performance to increase the likelihood of greater success in the future.

7.4.1 THE OBJECTIVES FOR YOU

- You are demonstrating empathy and the performer knows you understand their point of view.
- You are clear on their goals and objectives.
- You have given your feedback to a performer, who is now in a willing state to receive and use it.

- You have helped identify the learning that comes from every experience but which is often ignored or overlooked.
- You know what your performer is planning as their next step or goal.
- You know where, and how, you can offer your support, if needed, to ensure likelihood of success, and when to review progress.
- You have a framework for regular and spontaneous conversations.

The objectives for the performer are:

7.4.2 THE OBJECTIVES FOR THE PERFORMER

- Clarity on how they are getting on!
- Clarity on the objectives that they are aiming for.
- More enthusiasm as progress is identified and future possibilities discussed.
- Greater experience acknowledged, leading to a positive shift in self-belief.
- More choices for future actions leading to a feeling of greater control.
- Agreed next step that meets business expectations and personal needs.

The huge bonus for using a coaching circle is that it doesn't matter whether you've got ten minutes or an hour and a half. "I've got no time!" is no excuse because, as long as you have a few minutes to talk to someone, you've got time to focus their attention towards the next action which they know you'll be following up on! Here's how it works:

Ask your Gen Z employee to describe the ultimate objective for their performance. If you are reviewing an earlier performance, ask them to describe it "as if" it had gone perfectly, and the goal for the event had been achieved.

7.4.3 THE PERFORMANCE/ OBJECTIVE (A)

To encourage this level of creativity ask for more detail for their imagination to work on. The more detail they give you the more intense their "picture" of the ideal event. Even after the event is over, this "mental re-creation" helps the subconscious to identify with, and then to believe, the possibility of this goal being achievable.

Whenever you ask questions about their original goal it may become obvious that the performer themselves had not been clear before taking the action you are now reviewing.

As they describe their "ideal" performance, listen for what they think is important to them about it. You are bringing out some goals that they may not have expressed so clearly before.

You are in the emotion changing business. That's where their passion comes from and their commitment to all their actions. How are they feeling as they describe their "ideal" performance – their goal for the performance you are now reviewing? Expect to see more animation, more aliveness, more energy as they picture their goal.

Notice how you are feeling as you listen to their description – if you feel flat, the chances are that they are too. Can you lift their emotions up a notch before moving around the circle? Capture a bit more passion. Ask: "Imagine you had achieved this goal; where would that now allow you to go on to?" By lifting it up a level you discover what is really the source of inspiration for the performer. Here's an example:

Performer:	"I want to run an effective meeting that everyone thinks is worthwhile attending." (A worthy goal but not very exciting.)
Manager:	"Imagine you do run effective meetings, where would that allow you to go?"
Performer:	"I'd be able to spend more time working on a special project."
Manager:	"What will that special project give you?"
Performer:	"My own profit centre which might mean my own department one day."
Manager:	"So you see yourself one day running your own profitable department or division here or in a company like this?"
Performer:	"Yes, definitely – one day!"
Manager:	"So your immediate goal is to feel effective in running meetings?"

With the emotion level raised, we move on to B.

We've now got a frame of reference for evaluating the performance or whatever the situation is that you are talking about. Remember their emotions will be affected by their recollections. Your aim is to have them feeling better about themselves, after talking things over with you, than they felt beforehand. Some managers achieve precisely the opposite effect!

7.4.4 THE EVENT/ REVIEW (B)

Point them in the direction of the observations that are likely to give them a good feeling about themselves. "Tell me, what worked?" and get a list of examples where they can identify value in what they achieved. If you have been present during the same performance, point out things that impressed you.

It's the "half-bottle full, half-bottle empty" routine because most feedback falls into one of these two halves. The fuller a "half" becomes, the more energy there will be for making changes. Never let the balance fall the other way, however justified you feel it to be. Self-esteem, energy and certainly passion may drain away fast.

Then ask the question "What might have gone better – or what didn't work so well?" and help them identify one or two areas for improvement or change. If you were involved in the event, what did you notice that may need attention? Offer your feedback and perspective. Between the two of you, you will generate considerable feedback – there's always more but that need not be vital. They can now identify changes or modifications that will add to their commitment for improvement.

This process is continuous – there will be another review later. Anything missed will be picked up then.

7.4.5 THE LEARNING (C) Ask "What was one thing you learned from that 'event'?" It doesn't matter if it was a triumph or a disaster, there will be something useful to learn. Even a couple of learning points are enough to pull out. Then recognise what they have learned, positive and negative. The learning that they acknowledge to themselves can be worth as much as the experience of their performance. Recognising and valuing the learning needs of employees is a way of showing that you value them. It's important not to overlook or underestimate the significance of meeting this need for Gen Z individuals.

When you ignore the learning and merely judge them on whether their performance was successful or not by your criteria, you devalue an important asset of your organisation. By recognising and supporting the learning aspirations of Gen Z, employers can demonstrate their commitment to their growth and contribute to a more engaged and fulfilled workforce.

This part of the process is where the performer reviews the choices and makes a decision to take action or make a change. In order to narrow the focus and to make a choice of action realistic the next question is:

7.4.6 THE ACTION/PLAN (D)

- *What do you feel you might want to do first to get a better result?*

Have you ever asked a question like that of somebody who is feeling low and depressed and wants your advice? When you do ask this question the reply may be "I don't know!" However, if you have succeeded with the goal of having them feel better about themselves, you may have a completely different answer. One or two plans, however modest, will reset their progress towards a goal.

As they make their choice, you will want to be convinced that they will carry it out. Here are some questions to cement the certainty of action:

7.4.7 FROM PLAN TO PERFORMANCE

- *What will you do to develop your performance in this area?*
- *What's the first thing you want to do?*
- *When will you do that?* (Generally it should be within two weeks to take advantage of the impetus gained from the discussion!)
- *What obstacles could prevent you from taking that action?* (Better to acknowledge the obstacles

now, than to hear about them later when they are called excuses!)

Getting around an obstacle may become the first agreed step. How confident are they at taking the step they've chosen, whether it works or not, say on a scale of one to ten? Any score except a ten reveals a hidden obstacle or doubt. Is the action too challenging? Is there a smaller, easier one to start with?

Finally...

- *How can I support you?*
- *Is there anything you need from me by way of back up?*
- *When shall we meet again to review progress?*

When you use a coaching circle you make sure everyone keeps their focus – and keeps moving forward. Try it on yourself and reflect on a recent event. It will work for you too, on your own performance!

NB: A coaching circle is a perfect template for a verbal or written report for any performer to submit to their manager!

7.5 THOUGHTS FOR ACTION

Take a moment to pay attention to how often people in your environment give and receive feedback. Is it something that happens a lot, or is it rare? Also, think about the kind of feedback that is given. Is it mostly judgmental, where people are criticised or praised, or is it descriptive, focused on specific details and observations?

- *Is the person who is receiving feedback actively involved in the process, or do they feel like others are forcing it upon them? Do they take ownership of their own growth and learning?*
- *Consider how the feedback makes the person feel emotionally. Does it motivate and excite them to improve, or does it make them feel less enthusiastic?*

Noticing these things helps to better understand how feedback is valued in your environment and the impact it has on the Gen Z team member and on the company culture.

The question "How am I getting on?", if not resolved, causes a significant leak of potential, passion, energy and commitment. It can also lead to resistance to change.

By now they know how they are getting on, the next question that everyone asks themselves, but the leader rarely hears, is...

"Am I happy with what I am getting out of this...?"

Only when your consciousness is totally focused on the moment you are in can you receive whatever gift, lesson or delight that moment has to offer.

Barbara de Angelis

Question Eight

Am I Happy with What I'm Getting Out of This...?

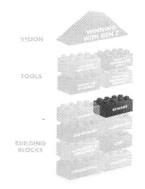

What motivates people to take on a new job? What motivates them to stay? What motivates them to take on more responsibility? What motivates them to stay late and finish a job? What motivates them to be adaptable, to contribute new ideas and to challenge conventional wisdom? What motivates them to do anything that you, as team leader, value and feel will contribute to the objectives of the team and the organisation?

The answer is straightforward.

It lies in the confidence of knowing that what they stand to gain, as a reward for their efforts, will fulfil their own unique requirements, needs and wants, whatever they may be. That is the real contract that governs whether people ration their energy, passion and creativity or offer them in abundance in a state of determination, dedication and joy!

DOI: 10.4324/9781003475613-8

Managers and team leaders must be aware of exactly what it is that people want from their job and commit themselves to ensuring that they can get it.

8.1 WHO CONTROLS THE REWARDS?

Many managers and team leaders believe it is their job to motivate their people. But that belief leads them into difficult territory. Why? Because it's an impossible brief. Motivation, for the most part, is a self-driven force that individuals cultivate within themselves. This happens when what they are doing is connected to their values and goals. A manager's role, therefore, is to make sure that you create an environment that encourages this connection and self-motivation. That's quite a different responsibility.

The two types of reward are the ones we give ourselves and the ones we get from other people – the intrinsic and the extrinsic.[1] The difference is huge! When your Gen Z employees pursue an intrinsic reward, they are in control. They decide themselves what it will be, the value it has to them and what they will do to get it. When they pursue an extrinsic reward, they may not enjoy so much control. Other people dictate what the reward will be and what they must do to get it. Others will even decide what value it will have. The motivational power is outside the performer, and the effect is more limited. Research even shows that contingent rewards – if you do this… then you'll get that – have a negative impact on motivation as it takes away some of the employee's autonomy.[2]

1 Extrinsic rewards are tangible, covering pay, bonuses and benefits. Intrinsic rewards are the psychological benefits each employee gains from making a meaningful contribution through their work.
2 Pink, D. (2009). *Drive: The Surprising Truth about What Motivates Us*. Conongate.

The extrinsic rewards can look alluring. In many cases, organisations and employees believe that these are the only motivators to ensure commitment and loyalty. These include money, bonuses, promotion, status, certificates, cars, shares and perks. And today, financial stability for Gen Z is even more sensitive than for previous generations. Given that over 50% of Gen Z individuals are living pay cheque to pay cheque, financial rewards play a crucial and immediate role in addressing these concerns.[3] Hoping to pay off student loans, to buy houses, plan for families and lay down permanent roots are presenting more challenging aspirations than ever. As the cost of living keeps on climbing with the uncertainty of enjoying continuing and stable employment, extrinsic rewards have a pressing relevance in the short term.

You can help your team members to see the connection with their intrinsic motivation and their financial remuneration. Intrinsic rewards, however, don't pay the rent!

Invite them to structure how their own productivity goals could earn more rewards in bonuses, incentives, commission and prizes. Setting goals, overcoming uncertainty, taking action and achieving the results they want within their control create confidence for navigating the more challenging target of negotiating increases in salary.

There is a vital role for you as their manager to play and take the lead in initiating these discussions. When you do, encourage them to share their thoughts on whether they perceive their pay is in line with

---

3 Deloitte (2023) Gen Z and Millennial survey 2023.

industry standards. They will have an opinion on this, since platforms like Glassdoor.com and Salary.com are making salary information easily accessible for everyone.

Unequal pay has been proven to disengage employees,[4] so it makes sense to prioritise this issue. Share the company's pay and benefits philosophy. Do what you can to influence it and review it regularly to make sure salary packages are competitive and at least reflect the cost of living. It matters as it directly affects their sense of value within the organisation. If they feel their pay is unjust, it will impact their engagement, diverting their energy towards feelings of disappointment and being undervalued.

When your Gen Z feels their pay is justified, the extrinsic rewards will become less important and your team members will start looking, even unconsciously, for other kinds of rewards, the self-motivating ones.

My name is Karen. Ari, one of my team, who joined our company as a technician, clearly had potential as a manager. He was very good at his job, worked well with colleagues, always exploring and coming up with new ideas and concepts independently and delivering great results.

I planned to train him and promote him to a more senior position. Being a part of Gen Z, like many of our new employees, we knew he had expectations of making an impact and I expected him to have ideas on his career progression. In our discussions, Ari expressed his ambition, and he told me that he needed higher pay to give him some freedom to pay back debts, save for a deposit on an apartment, have time for voluntary work in his leisure time and still enjoy himself!

---

4 Pink, D. (2009). *Drive: The Surprising Truth about What Motivates Us.* Conongate.

Despite the promise of extra money, he didn't seem too happy about leaving a job he so enjoyed.

Together we explored the options. We didn't want him to leave, but his job grade limited further pay increases. And equally we didn't want to risk promoting someone to a post where they may not be so effective.

Prompted by this challenge we created a new job with more responsibility. Whilst still practising his skills as a technician he would be responsible for training standards and working closely with his non- technical manager to present new ideas to senior colleagues. He would learn first-hand about the technical challenges at every level of the company and work with the manager and the team to offer solutions.

His increasing experience was being valued and rewarded and his profile was enhanced. He could see career pathways opening up. Ari is still with us, now working in a newly created research division.

Director, Sustainable Energy Company

8.2 THE QUESTIONS THAT WILL MAKE ALL THE DIFFERENCE

Do they want job satisfaction, personal growth, learning, enhanced self-image and self-worth, pride, security, freedom, a feeling of contribution?

Discussing what people really want from their work allows the possibility for the rewards to come from a variety of sources and not necessarily the one that is targeted. In light of this, consider the flexibility and customisation of your benefits and rewards programme. This way, you can ensure there's something for every generation and preference, creating a more inclusive and appealing package for your diverse team.

To start this conversation you can simply ask your team the following question:

- *What's really important to you about your work?*

A fairly general question but it invites a brainstorming list of all the values that they connect with work. These are the ones that give a sense of elevating self-worth and are the evidence that there is satisfaction, enjoyment and reward in their work. Within a few minutes their list might look something like this:

- challenges
- doing new things
- healthy work/life balance
- time off to do volunteering or travelling
- security
- the money
- working with others
- career progression
- being creative
- achieving goals
- improving skills
- the experience
- the perks

Then invite each member of the team separately to select five or six from the list in the priority of importance to them. Follow up with asking them to score out of ten the degree to which that benefit or reward is motivating them or is seen to be achievable in their job right now.

Together you'll have a clear idea of the shortfalls that may be inhibiting them from bringing all their energies to achieving their own and the company's goals and objectives. However, what we wouldn't learn, and couldn't guess at with this question, is what those shortfalls specifically mean for that individual employee.

It's the next question that gets the significant needs out in the open. These are the ones, if noticeably lacking, which can inhibit enthusiasm, creativity and self-responsibility. With this awareness you, as the manager, can be enabled to direct your efforts towards helping that employee find more meaning in their work.

- *What would need to be happening if that reward (what you feel is important) was motivating you to a higher degree than it is presently?*

With this question they are invited to use their imagination, to leap forward in time and create a picture of what they are seeing, hearing and feeling that will describe the answer. For example, if the reward being discussed was "personal development" the evidence might be "running my own project team and reporting directly to the customer". This then offers huge potential for you to guide your team members towards this objective. If they are ready for the responsibility and there is an opportunity, maybe that could be arranged sooner rather than later? If they are not ready, then a development programme can be created with the eventual leadership of a project team being the agreed objective.

This kind of approach is essential for Gen Z as they are looking for personalised benefits and rewards to fit the broader context of their lives and what they are hoping to achieve. Through this exploration, you will uncover the nuances that shape their perspectives on workplace compensation, health benefits, insurance and pension schemes, professional development and training, flexible working and work–life balance.

8.2.1 QUESTIONS TO ASK YOURSELF

- *What can I and our business do to meet these needs?*
- *What role is HR playing in this and how can the rewards and benefits on offer become visible, understandable and explained to our Gen Z employees?*

8.3 WHAT ARE THE REAL MOTIVATORS?

Pay alone won't create the enduring, positive motivation that elevates their passion, energy and creativity that they can bring to the organisation. The workplace is an ideal arena where the influence of these aspirations can be exercised, harnessed and nurtured. Those who bring their true selves, the self that is passionate, energetic and mindful, seek a link between their role at work and their personal values. This is the secret that fosters long-lasting engagement and dedication and this is very important to Gen Z.

Stephen Covey sums it up perfectly in his book *The Seven Habits of Highly Effective People.*[5] He identifies the real motivators as: to love, to live, to learn and to leave a legacy.

These encapsulate and highlight the essence of our existential purpose and the worth of our life's achievements.

8.3.1 TO LOVE

"To love" involves feeling a meaningful connection with one's work, colleagues, customers and suppliers.

- *What's important to you about your job?*
- *What gives it meaning to you?*
- *What do you value from the people you work with?*

---

5 Covey, S. (2013). *The Seven Habits of Highly Effective People*, Simon & Schuster.

Recognising the good in others brings rewards to every work-related relationship.

"To live" means experiencing life fully – setting and achieving goals, and being happy and successful both in the workplace and beyond.

8.3.2 TO LIVE

- *What are you seeking to achieve at work and in other spheres of your life?*
- *What are your measures of success in the workplace?*
- *What new things have you done recently in our organisation?*

Acknowledging present accomplishments and personal values.

"To learn" is to experience growth and to identify real progress.

8.3.3 TO LEARN

- *What did you learn from that last performance?*
- *What will you do differently next time?*
- *What do you want to target as your next learning opportunity?*

Exploring possibilities for continual and never-ending learning.

"To leave a legacy" involves knowing that your contribution leaves something better behind. It may be modified later, but you, and your input, made future changes possible.

8.3.4 TO LEAVE A LEGACY

- *What processes are you putting in place that will free you up for other challenges?*

- *What will be the main difference that you feel responsible for making?*
- *What's the vision ultimately that you are moving towards, and how is your part in that adding unique value?*

Revealing the ultimate reward. You made a difference!

When individuals are denied opportunities to live, love, learn and leave a legacy, it is likely that their work becomes either a flurry of activity under pressure or uninspiringly boring. Life becomes filled with trying to deal with mistakes, problems and crises and blaming events that they deny having any control of and complaining about the shortcomings of other people.

Work will be viewed as the source of their frustration, where its only meaning is the pay cheque. Every one of the eight questions covered in this book, the questions we are all likely to ask ourselves but bosses are rarely aware of, speaks to these four main motivators. They resonate for a lifetime and bring to each of us our own rewards.

What will this really mean?

- It's rewarding for Gen Z.
- It's rewarding for everyone who works with you.
- It's rewarding for the reputation and achievements of your organisation.

Happiness brings its own rewards. Of all the arenas in our lives, the workplace, wherever it exists, offers us a stimulating framework for continuing our journey of personal growth, leading us to achieve whatever we really deserve in our lives.

And Finally,

We were inspired to write this book because whenever the subject of Gen Z was mentioned it was usually followed by a negative judgement, even when one was not invited.

We would hear:

> difficult, arrogant, lazy, overly ambitious, not ambitious enough, easily upset and intimidated, reluctant to speak without being forewarned, pushing for changes to traditional practices with zero experience, addicted to their 'phones, preferring texting to speaking, determination to work from home and generally critical of what has gone before, both in and out of the workplace.

We knew these descriptions were wildly mis-placed. We know many Gen Zers who don't remotely match these characteristics. We know many businesses who are successfully recruiting Gen Z and benefiting from their talents.

The media, and anecdotal observers, rarely promote all the positive attributes these Gen Zs bring to our lives. Are we told that they are highly collaborative, self-reliant, pragmatic, adaptable, have unparalleled technological prowess, an entrepreneurial spirit, collective problem-solving skills, awareness of the significance and added value of diversity and inclusion, are future focused, hungry to learn and develop and have the energy and the vision to see better possibilities for the greater good of everyone? Plus the energy and commitment to see changes through to acceptance and conclusion.

In the workplace, Gen Z meet and interact with other generations. Here, where they will be working and collaborating with everyone, is where they are most likely to realise their potential. Their questions, and yours, will deliver the building blocks that create a strong and enduring collaboration. They will learn and grow as they contribute to your business success whilst simultaneously influencing and expanding all our future horizons.

Gen Z really do hold the key to all our future prospects.

The questions in this book, as straightforward as they are, are a key to unlocking their power. Each question you ask, your commitment to listen, your willingness to explore and support new ideas and action will super-charge the energy Gen Z bring.

They are going to make a big difference....and so will you. Any more questions?

Anna and Peter

Questions by Chapter

QUESTION 1: DO I REALLY UNDERSTAND WHAT IS EXPECTED OF ME....?

THE CHALLENGE: KNOWING WHOSE EXPECTATION IT IS? (page 5)

- *What would your team, your customer and your suppliers, internal and external, say if you asked them about their expectations of you?*
- *How long has it been since you last asked them? What might have changed?*
- *What would be the evidence that you understand exactly what is expected of you?*
- *How would you know, in one year, that you've done a good job?*

ASKING QUESTIONS TO CONFIRM UNDERSTANDING (page 7)

- *Where do you expect to be on this project by, say, the end of the month?*
- *What is your plan for supporting the team's goals?*
- *What could prevent you from delivering the results you promised?*
- *What are your customers and colleagues expecting to achieve from your activity?*
- *Exactly how may I support you?*
- *What do you want to do first to move this forward?*
- *What do you want to focus on once you've achieved the first objective?*

LIVING THE VALUES OF THE ORGANISATION (page 8)

- *What behaviours are you noticing in the organisation/team/department?*
- *What value is being expressed from what you notice?*
- *Is that what we want to express? If so, how is it linked to our company values and strategy? If not, what behaviours would you like to be observing and experiencing?*
- *What does it look like when we're demonstrating the value of, say, integrity and ethics, respect, innovation, drive, trust, etc. [insert your own values] in our company/team?*
- *How do we support each other to practise our values and how do we speak up when company/ team decisions and behaviours aren't in line?*
- *How do we communicate our values to our customers, both verbally and through actions?*
- *What part do our values play in our recruitment and promotion decisions?*

AND FINALLY, SOME MORE QUESTIONS FOR YOU TO ASK YOURSELF... (page 10)

- *Do you know what is expected of you in your role as a manager or a team leader? On a score of one to ten? Identify what would be different if the score was higher. What actions would make a difference to how you rate yourself? Verify expectations with customers, other departments, your own boss and your team.*
- *What aspects of your leadership and support, your work approach, and the service you provide, are important to your team?*
- *Does your team really know what's expected of them?*

QUESTION 2: DO I KNOW WHY IT IS EXPECTED OF ME...?

OWNING AND COMMUNICATING THE ORGANISATION'S PURPOSE (page 17)

- *What is our organisation's purpose and objectives and what are the team's purpose and objectives?*
- *How does our purpose relate to the goals we've all agreed and the numbers we're keeping an eye on?*
- *How would others recognise what differentiates our team, our organisation, our products and services?*
- *What makes our company unique on an emotional level? What does each member of the team think and feel? Are they inspired?*
- *What would we be doing if we had the reputation of being the best team in our industry?*
- *How can I, as a part of the team, support the team to turn our purpose from words into actions and behaviours?*

GEN Z BRINGS A DIFFERENCE (page 20)

- *What makes each of our team members unique in their job and where do they add value (both knowledge and financially) to our organisation?*
- *How is our commitment to diversity benefiting our company's bottom line?*
- *How and where is each person's contribution and perspective acknowledged and appreciated?*
- *How does valuing DEIB express the company's purpose and lead to more job satisfaction as everyone understands not only what is expected of them but why?*

WHAT DOES YOUR "CUSTOMER" REALLY WANT? (page 21)

- *What are your key frustrations in dealing with people like us, or products or services like ours?*
- *How are your Gen Z team members serving their colleagues?*
- *How are your Gen Z members being served?*

FINALLY, SOME MORE QUESTIONS TO ASK YOURSELF... (page 22)

- *Do you understand WHY you are doing what's expected of you as a manager? On a scale of one to ten, how effectively does your day to day work connect to the bigger picture and the company's purpose?*
- *Identify what would be different if the score was higher. What actions could you take that would make a difference?*
- *How can you support your team members to connect their roles to the organisation's vision and purpose?*
- *What can you do to keep drawing out the big picture and challenge everyone to bring fresh views to every meeting?*

QUESTION 3: *DO I AGREE...?*

AGREEMENT BEFORE INITIAL RECRUITMENT (page 26)

- *Where have you experienced feelings of pride at work?*
- *When have you felt that your work is more meaningful to you than at other times?*
- *Where have you recognised a match between our company's purpose and mission and what you think is important in your life?*

- *When in your life, either at work or elsewhere, have you failed to achieve what you wanted, disappointed yourself and accepted that another succeeded where you did not?*
- *What did you learn from these events and how did you change your approach to the next similar situation?*
- *How do you think that what's expected of you will bring greater benefits to both you and to the organisation?*
- *What support could we offer that would make you feel confident to maximise your energies, initiative and creativity in pursuing and achieving the objectives of our organisation?*

Be prepared for them to ask you:

- *What are your organisation's values and purpose (though they should have done some research!)?*
- *In practice how do you expect these to be demonstrated in your daily interactions with colleagues and customers?*
- *Is there a difference between how colleagues are treated and the attitude shown to customers?*
- *What are examples of the career trajectories of colleagues in your organisation and what support did they receive in achieving their success?*
- *How will I know how I am getting on so that I can maximise my experience and learning?*
- *What are your protocols for meeting the work-life balance aspirations of everyone in the organisation?*
- *Whom may I speak to, in a similar role, who can tell me a little more about what it's like working here, from their perspective?*

GETTING INTO THE "FLOW STATE" (page 29)

- *To what degree do they feel the task has meaning for them?*
- *Are the goals for the task crystal clear?*
- *Is the task appropriately challenging?*
- *What measures are in place to minimise interference?*
- *To what degree is there freedom as to how the task should be delivered?*

HOW DO YOU KNOW IF THEY AGREE, REALLY AGREE? (page 31)

- *On a scale of one to ten, if ten is your highest sense of agreeing with what's expected of you, where do you rate how you feel right now?*
- *If your score was one number higher what would be different?*

QUESTION 4: *WHO CARES...?*

WHAT MATTERS TO GEN Z? (page 35)

- *What activities do you enjoy outside the workplace? Would you appreciate time off instead of bonuses or pay for overtime as recognition for exceptional results?*
- *How well do we notice others' feelings, and do we pick up clues that could lead to constructive and positive discussions?*
- *In what instances does displaying kindness boost engagement, while the presence of intolerance serves as a demotivator?*
- *Are we ready to set aside biases, and values that might lead to disagreement and discord by influencing workplace decisions?*

- *Are we aware of the impact of mental wellbeing within the company? Eg is there an appreciation of the difference between 'being anxious' which is commonplace and 'anxiety' which can be a debilitating condition?*
- *With new ways of working, which may lead to more solitary work, is there active encouragement for value-adding face to face meetings and team gatherings?*

WHERE IS THE 'CARE' IN YOUR MEETINGS? (page 38)

- *Do you declare your purpose for the meeting and get agreement at the beginning?*
- *Do you ask everyone for their 'intended outcome,' what they want from their time spent in the meeting both for themselves and for the organisation, and do you share yours?*
- *Do you invite members to switch off their phones, email notifications, and laptops (when appropriate) or ideally leave them outside the room to allow participants to be fully present and actively participate?*
- *Do you make sure that all participants, including Gen Z, have a voice in the meeting?*
- *Do you check on a time schedule that suits everyone and stick to it even if the entire agenda is not completed?*
- *At the end of the meeting do you ask whether 'intended outcomes' have been achieved?*
- *To improve the quality of future meetings, do you ask: "What worked?" "What could have worked better?" And apply the learning at future meetings?*

CARING MEANS BETTER RESULTS! (page 41)

- *How much do you enjoy yourself in your work?*
- *Imagine that you are now in the future and that your score is just one point higher. What is now happening that wasn't happening before that makes you feel that work is a little bit more enjoyable?*
- *What might be a first step, however small, that you could take to move towards the situation that you would really like?"*

QUESTION 5: BUT CAN I DO IT...?

Questions to ask yourself: (page 46)

- *Do they look for excuses to explain a failure to deliver what is expected of them?*
- *Do they detach themselves from their agreed responsibility to carry out the task effectively?*
- *Do they identify and consider alternative choices of action or procrastinate and end up doing nothing?*
- *Do they look for someone else to do it for them?*
- *Do they go quiet and into their shell?*
- *Are they reluctant to take an initial step that may not be part of a previously accepted process for fear it won't work or be approved.*
- *Do they have access to the necessary resources and support to accomplish the task successfully?*
- *If the task is a new challenge for them, is there a back up plan in place to support their intention in the event of a loss of direction or an unforeseen obstacle?*
- *Has the task, and their role in achieving a successful outcome, been discussed and agreed*

by the individual, the team, and me as the manager?

- *Have I involved them in the task assignment process, allowing them to express any preferences or concerns?*
- *What support, if any, will they need?*
- *When will they deliver what they promise? Is this agreed?*
- *What learning do they want to achieve from this new experience?*

STARTING AT THE WRONG END (page 49)

- *What are you thinking and believing about yourself and about this situation, expectation or challenge? Is this true and helpful?*
- *If there is a negative and limiting belief what would have to be different, and in your control, for you to believe that you can do this?*
- *What would be a first step that you could take that would be in your control?*
- *What is a positive learning from past events that you can apply this time?*

FOCUS ON PROCESS (page 50)

- *What did you notice about the process?*
- *What worked for you, where could it have worked better? Are there changes that might be considered?*
- *What have you learned about the process and about yourself?*
- *What will you do differently in the next similar situation?*
- *What do we all agree is our process for each task, our team's way of 'doing it', the process that will produce the results that we are here to deliver?*

PLAY TO STRENGTH (page 51)

- *What skills or abilities do you believe set you apart and contribute significantly to the team's success?*
- *When faced with challenges, what strengths do you rely on to navigate and overcome them successfully?*
- *Are there specific tasks or projects where you feel you bring a unique perspective or skill set that others might not have?*
- *Reflecting on positive feedback you've received, what strengths or qualities are frequently highlighted?*

TRAINING AND DEVELOPMENT (page 51)

- *Agree with the team member what it is they want to learn on a course or workshop, or from a colleague, and where they will apply their new knowledge and with what beneficial effect – ideally in 'bottom line' terms.*
- *Review the key learning points after the course and agree to a plan whereby the team member uses the new knowledge on purpose and with regular supportive reviews and feedback from you as their manager.*
- *A final review after six months to assess progress and competence – and to put a bottom-line value on the difference that using the new skill is making.*

WHEN THE PROBLEM SEEMS TO BE OUTSIDE THEIR CONTROL (page 52)

- *What options do you have to overcome these obstacles that you haven't yet tried?*

- *What will you do first and what support do you need?*
- *What is the picture you can imagine, once the obstacle is no longer in the way, that shows you are one step closer to your goal?*
- *What would have to be different to enable this thing you want to happen, to actually happen?*
- *Which of these things/events/people can you begin to influence? What difference would that make?*
- *Which do you want to choose first to take action on in order to move towards your goal?*
- *When will you do that and what support, if any, do you need?*
- *When can we catch up and review where you are and how you are getting on?*

TEAM SPIRIT AND COLLABORATION (page 54)

- *Can we do what is expected of us?*
- *What obstacles or problems might we encounter?*
- *What can we do differently to close the gap or gain an advantage?*
- *What do you see as our individual roles in overcoming an obstacle?*
- *What do we need to do in order to carry out our roles effectively?*
- *How have we confirmed what it is that others in the team are relying on us to deliver?*

QUESTION 6: *AM I CONFIDENT IN DOING WHAT'S EXPECTED OF ME...?*

- *How confident are you feeling, doing what is expected of you?*

REFRAMING NEGATIVE THOUGHTS (page 59)

INTERNALLY

- *What is happening, what am I noticing most, what is my intention, what is really true?*

EXTERNALLY

- *How are you feeling right now about your performance in your role?*
- *What are you noticing most that is giving you this feeling?*
- *What if you could change that thought or feeling, what would it be like? What would be happening?*
- *When you doubt your abilities, what evidence supports those doubts? What evidence contradicts them?*
- *With a changed perspective of the current situation, what would that mean to you, where could that take you?*
- *What steps could you take to move forward? What would you choose, however small, to be the first step?*
- *What support would you want from colleagues or me?*
- *When can we meet to review progress?*

HELP THEM EXPAND THEIR COMFORT ZONE (page 67)

- *Is there a particular area in the team or company that you're curious to explore or learn more about?*
- *Are there training programmes or workshops you believe would be beneficial for your career development?*

- *What gaps, if any, have you noticed in your experience, knowledge or skill set?*
- *In what ways can I support you in stepping outside your Comfort Zone and taking on new challenges?*

QUESTION 7: *HOW AM I GETTING ON...?*

MAKING FEEDBACK TRULY VALUABLE (page 72)

- *Ideally, what were you intending to achieve?*
- *How did you feel about that performance?*
- *What did you notice about it?*
- *What did you learn from it?*
- *If you were able to do it again, what would you do differently?*

FROM PLAN TO PERFORMANCE (page 81)

- *What will you do to develop your performance in this area?*
- *What's the first thing you want to do?*
- *When will you do that? (Generally it should be within two weeks to take advantage of the impetus gained from the discussion!)*
- *What obstacles could prevent you from taking that action? (Better to acknowledge the obstacles now, than to hear about them later when they are called excuses!)*
- *How can I support you?*
- *Is there anything you need from me by way of back up?*
- *When shall we meet again to review progress?*

THOUGHTS FOR ACTION (page 82)

- *Is the person who is receiving feedback actively involved in the process, or do they feel like others are forcing it upon them? Do they take ownership of their own growth and learning?*

- *Consider how the feedback makes the person feel emotionally. Does it motivate and excite them to improve, or does it make them feel less enthusiastic?*

QUESTION 8: *AM I HAPPY WITH WHAT I'M GETTING OUT OF THIS...?*

THE QUESTIONS THAT WILL MAKE ALL THE DIFFERENCE *(page 89)*

- *What's really important to you about your work?*
- *What would need to be happening if that reward (what you feel is important) was motivating you to a higher degree than it is presently?*

Questions to ask yourself:

- *What can I and our business do to meet these needs?*
- *What role is HR playing in this and how can the rewards and benefits on offer become visible, understandable and explained to our Gen Z employees?*

WHAT ARE THE REAL MOTIVATORS? *(page 92)*

TO LOVE

- *What's important to you about your job?*
- *What gives it meaning to you?*
- *What do you value from the people you work with?*

TO LIVE

- *What are you seeking to achieve at work and in other spheres of your life?*
- *What are your measures of success in the workplace?*
- *What new things have you done recently in our organisation?*

TO LEARN

- *What did you learn from that last performance?*
- *What will you do differently next time?*
- *What do you want to target as your next learning opportunity?*

TO LEAVE A LEGACY

- *What processes are you putting in place that will free you up for other challenges?*
- *What will be the main difference that you feel responsible for making?*
- *What's the vision ultimately that you are moving towards, and how is your part in that adding unique value?*

We learn more by looking for the answer to a question, and not finding it, than we do from learning the answer itself.

Lloyd Alexander

Appendix I

Leader as Coach

The eight questions in this book offer a framework by which leaders can assess their personal effectiveness both as a coach and as an inspiring manager. You can use it in different ways to assess your level of effectiveness as a leader in a project, managing a team member or during a period of organisational change.

Together, these questions raise awareness of the building blocks of self-motivation and engagement. These are the questions that performers ask themselves but the leaders rarely hear.

From each answer, strategies will evolve that will enable you, as leader and coach, to create high-performance environments for you and your team. These will be the platforms from which great results are sought and achieved.

A simple self-assessment will let you know how effective you feel you are now and indicate the possibilities for closer collaboration leading to greater aspiration and commitment for everyone in your team.

EACH OF THE EIGHT QUESTIONS HAS THREE MEASURES

1. How important do you feel this question is in the area of self-motivation and engagement? Very – 10, Not at all – 0.
2. How effective are you in raising and discussing this question? Very – 10, Not at all – 0.
3. How often do you focus your attention on this question? Regularly – 10, Not at all – 0.

You will have a starting point from which to further develop your leadership and coaching skills.

On a scale of 0 to 10 to what degree:		How important is this question for self-motivation and engagement?	How effective are you in raising it?	How often do you focus your attention on it?
1.	Do they really understand what is expected of them?			
2.	Do they know why this is expected of them?			
3.	Does it align with what they want to be doing?			
4.	Do they know who cares?			
5.	Do they know how to do what is expected of them?			
6.	Are they confident in doing what's expected of them?			
7.	Do they know how they are getting on?			
8.	Do they feel that their rewards are appropriate and satisfying?			
	Score out of 80	/80	/80	/80

If your score exceeds 60 in each column, you are very aware of the factors that motivate people. Creating a high-performing environment is a major part of your leadership strategy.

If your score is over say 45, you have an awareness of the factors that motivate people. Are there some missed opportunities?

If your score falls below say 20, there could be reserves of energy, passion and commitment that your team or team members are not bringing to work. You might be missing out on some opportunities for growth and success.

The Evolving Generations

Throughout the twentieth century and into the present one, commentators, writers, politicians and marketeers have grouped every year into definable segments, and given each one a title. A concept that began in the United States is now widely adopted throughout most Western societies. These groupings, known as Generations, have provided a convenient "box" into which to place all society's aspirations, behaviours, political traits, investments, technology, inventions, discoveries and concerns, so that they can be recognised, explained and attributed to. They become the influential generation of the day.

These divisions are not an exact science and they overlap considerably. They are, however, a guide that influences marketing strategies, government policies, investment decisions and business priorities. The trend has been for each generation to span ever decreasing years whilst each makes an increasing impact on society.

Every generation tends to be dismissive of the previous one and be suspicious and critical of the next one. And so it goes on!

They all make changes, or are changed, in ways that reflect how they experienced their upbringing and how they choose to live their lives. Each current generation who holds the levers of power find they have to adapt their conviction of how their world works in order to accommodate and absorb the increasing influence of the next one.

A predominant area of our lives that impacts us all is the world of work. The circumstances which envelope the experiences of youth give generations different views on the priorities of their position in the workplace. It heavily influences what they expect, what is expected of them and their obligations to earn a living.

Flexibility by both employers and employees is now more challenging than ever. In whatever way future generations see the world and their place in it, today it is the attitudes and behaviours of Gen Z that, for better or worse, are beginning to make the biggest impact on our society.

1. The Greatest Generation (Born 1901–1924)

THE SEVEN GENERATIONS

This is originally an American concept of labelling generations; this generation was brought up during the Great Depression through to the increasing threat of a world war. They value hard work, loyalty and traditional values. They went on to fight for freedom in World War II.

They had a strong sense of community and responsibility to their country and a respect for authority. They were interested in direct communication, so enjoyed speaking in person as opposed to via technology.

2.**The Silent Generation** (born 1925–1945)

They were brought up during a period of political unrest and World War II. They have a desire for stability and security. They were taught to be seen and not heard. Respect for authority is highly valued as well as loyalty to their employer.

3.**The Baby Boomers** (born 1946–1964)

They are so named because of the surge of births after World War II. They experienced significant societal changes including the civil rights and feminist movements, the Cold War and the formation of Soviet Russia, the Vietnam war and the anti-war movement and the Watergate scandal. There was a steadily increasing and strong economy, and teenagers were targeted as an identifiable new market. They came of age in the 1960s.

They espoused a strong desire for social change and progress. Baby Boomers were often labelled the "Me" generation as they were considered, at the time, more self-centred than previous generations. They were brought up to be competitive and self-sufficient and played a significant role in developing new technologies.

4.**Gen X** (born 1965–1980)

This generation straddles both the digital and non-digital world and understands the importance of both. They are considered sceptical of traditional values and institutions.

They were the first generation of "latchkey kids" as more women and mothers entered the workforce. They became more independent than previous generations and are known for their willingness to challenge authority and to think for themselves. They are resourceful, logical and good problem-solvers. The first generation to be brought up with widespread access to personal computers and the internet.

5.**The Millennials** (born 1981–1996)

Their coming of age bridged the global recession of 2008–2009, the terrorists acts of September 11 and the Iraq war. They faced a challenging job market. Many have looked for alternative ways to make a living such as starting their own business.

They are the first generation to make full and effective use of digital technology and to use the internet to solve their problems and to learn. They are generally highly educated and have been exposed to a wide range of ideas and perspectives. They seek employers who have flexible working practices and who espouse values which they consider important.

6.**Gen Z** (born 1997–2012)

They are confident and ambitious and continue expanding on trends promoted by the Millennials. They grew up entirely in the digital age but were severely impacted by the pandemic which interrupted their education and the social interactions of many. They are sometimes described as iGen but also labelled "screenagers" as they prefer communications to be via screens, smartphones, laptops and tablets over face-to-face conversations. They are more socially and politically aware than previous generations and tend to prioritise issues such as climate change, racial and gender equality and LGBTQ rights.

7.**Generation Alpha** (born 2013–2025)

This generation is even more digitally intuitive than Millennials and Gen Z. They are likely to be comfortable integrating AI into every aspect of life. They show indications of prioritising self-expression, self-reliance and personal fulfilment. Perhaps they will be more open minded and less likely to conform to traditional societal norms?

These generational differences, whilst never asserting themselves to be entirely accurate descriptions of individuals within each one, offer us insights into how humanity has evolved through time.

They can help us to know how we can best work differently with each group. How we co-create, co-design and collaborate with each other will depend upon respecting our differences. Together we can create a better society that benefits us all.

Appendix III

The Supplement

This book highlights the questions your team asks themselves, the questions you can ask the team and the questions you may be asking yourself. The questions apply to Gen Z as well as to everyone else in the workplace.

You ask questions in order for your performer to raise their awareness of everything they need to know in order for them to make informed decisions and to take responsibility for their consequent actions.

Questions are effective in the context of certainty that they can reveal natural abilities within the potential of any performer that can be applied to each new challenge or objective.

There is a framework for every journey we choose to undertake, geographically, at work or metaphorically.

FRAMING THE QUESTION

A frame for progress has signposts. Four, at least, are essential. They can be combined in any order or no order. Each signpost can be valuable on its own but together they form the bedrock of a safe and inevitable route to the destination we choose. This route is where the best decisions, taken in the moment, are made and where progress towards realising potential and achieving personal and business growth is made.

These four signposts are:

1. **The objectives** – *the destination.*
2. **The present position** – *where we are starting from.*
3. **The choices of possible routes**.
4. **The actions** – *the next steps to take to keep us on route, however challenging.*

OBJECTIVES

Purpose

1. using imagination to create pictures of eventual goals or improvement
2. developing more positive and exciting attitudes
3. clarity of objective shared, agreed and supported by others
4. creating a reference point for monitoring future progress

Tips

1. When the initial goal doesn't seem that exciting to the performer or coach, ask "Where would that take you eventually?" or "What would that mean to you?" Keep asking until the emotion is raised by identifying a more distant objective, however far off and vague that might be. Then return to focus on a short-term, early objective. Never dismiss or cast doubt on a long-term goal, however ambitious it may seem. If it excites, it will motivate. It needs no further justification.
2. Make sure that there is a congruent purpose – the needs of the performer and the team both being met.

3. Agree some critical success factors, or stepping stones – markers or measurements that can make the gap between the ends of the journey less daunting. Use numbers between 0 and 10 to aid measurement. If the ultimate goal is a 10, where would the performer want to be in 3 months? What number on the scale, and what would they be seeing, and hearing and feeling that would provide the evidence?
4. Don't worry if the ultimate goal is a bit fuzzy. It's the first stepping stone goal which needs to be specific, with a time scale on it.

Questions to ask:

- What does your objective look like, sound like, feel like? Where do you intend this will take you eventually? What's the bigger context for this issue?
- What's a first stage goal that is on the way?
- When do you want to achieve these goals?
- How will you measure progress?
- How does this objective meet your needs, the team's needs and the organisation's needs?

1. To generate feedback and awareness from as many perspectives as possible to identify exactly the present situation in an objective, non-judgemental and unbiased way.
2. To pinpoint the starting point from which choices may be made and which can be used as a reference point to evaluate progress.
3. To confirm recognition and value to a performer and encourage a positive attitude about the present position and their ability to take responsibility to move away from it.

PRESENT POSITION

Purpose

4. To identify the success factors which can be built upon, the limiting factors which can be changed and the obstacles which can be confronted and overcome.

Tips

1. Keep the focus of attention mainly on the factors that will enhance the self-efficacy of the performer (the feeling that the ability to create a change lies within the performer). That means that specific evidence that denotes progress or advantage should always outweigh but not preclude, the problems, set-backs or weaker areas.

2. Demonstrate empathy by listening to the performer's perspective. It is their truth though it might not be yours. Offer to contribute your perspective to fill out the whole picture.

3. Be aware of their emotional responses. If not positive and up-beat revisit objectives, confirm present value and identify obstacles to progress that they can influence. Do not go onto CHOICES until you are feeling positive that they want to proceed.

4. Use 0–10 measurements for agreeing a position, then seek evidence that justifies that score. (e.g. "You say you are about a 7 for feeling confident as a salesperson – what do you notice that contributes to that score? What evidence would tell you if you were at an 8?").

5. Ask for the performer's opinion of other people's perspectives about the issue. It invites more evidence in relative safety!

6. You are preparing to ask the performer for many choices of action. To make it easy to create

them, you need to have a prompt list under three headings:

i.   positive aspects for building upon
ii.   Less-developed aspects for remedial work
iii. obstacles now or in the future for confronting and surmounting

7. However much time you have allocated for discussion at least half should be spent on the first two steps, Objectives and Present Position. The more information generated the better and there is no limit to the detail available at both ends of the journey. Many conversations in business rush this stage to get on to "actions" which often have neither clear purpose nor agreed relevancy.

8. Listen for the opportunity to identify a sub-goal which could become a first stepping-stone goal (e.g. "You say your meetings are always chaotic, how does that affect your goal?"). It is normal to bounce between Objectives and Present Position until both ends of the journey are really established.

9. Remember it's what is important to them that needs to be brought out first and valued, before adding what's important to you! Though the facts are important, they are not as important as the underlying message being transmitted in this communication "You matter to me, the team and the organisation and I am committed to your success". You are focusing on people, not always functions or tasks!

10. Finally, reconfirm the goals, which may be modified or changed before moving on to CHOICES.

11. You want to encourage an exploration of now – not an explanation of it. Avoid asking "why" questions and encourage facts rather than justification by asking "What? When? Where? How much? How often?"

Questions to ask:

- Where would you score this issue right now on a scale of 0–10 if 10 is your objective? What are the positive aspects of the evidence? What is missing?
- How do you feel about this issue right now? What are you noticing that influences those feelings?
- What's generally working well and is a positive factor?
- What needs to change or be improved?
- What is the effect on others?
- What have you done about this so far and what was the effect?
- What's holding you back and what might be an obstacle in the future?

CHOICES Many performers struggling to resolve an issue feel that they have limited power and control and few choices to make and that the ultimate objective is possibly beyond their achievement and belief.

Purpose

1. To emphasise and confirm that whilst the entire journey cannot be pre- planned in convincing detail, a next step certainly can be selected and from a choice of many. Power, control and freedom are regained.
2. To generate many alternate choices for action, which can be drawn up as and when needed in the future.

3. To promote and value the creativity of the performer, inspired by the team (whether this team is just the boss/coach and performer or the larger team of colleagues).
4. Quantity rather than quality which allows for choices to include the previously rejected, the radical, the novel, the risky, the right-brained, the intuitive, the lateral thinking, the plainly obvious, the minority opinion, the junior's perception and the politically dangerous! A crazy idea might spark off a more useful one!
5. To listen.
6. To contribute your own ideas if invited.
7. To avoid wasting time on an irrelevant, though easy target. (E.g. The choice of working extra hours to boost productivity may mask another choice of improving communication between suppliers and production which may be more beneficial in the long term.)

1. Be aware of time restraints. Enough time must   ***Tips***
be reserved for final consideration and planning for implementation under ACTIONS.
2. Avoid lengthy discussion about one choice that may take away time from three, more original, ideas.
3. Never judge a choice. Just record it and ask for a next one. It is a brainstorm and not the final selection!
4. Refer back to Present Position for clues and prompts (e.g. "You mentioned earlier that your boss never volunteered feedback on your project, what could you do to address that?")

5. The more "obstacles" you identified earlier, the more choices there are for a first action.
6. Remove obvious restraints when seeking creativity by asking "What if?" questions e.g. "What if you had the influence of your boss, what could you do then?"

Questions to ask:

- What choices do you have?
- What could you do to address ......?
- What would you like to see happening that would give you more confidence?
- What if you had all the time you needed?
  - Were your boss?
  - Had enough money?
  - Had nothing else to do?
  - Had all the skill and ability?
  - Were your role-model?
- What has worked elsewhere?
- What can we learn from this challenge?

and finally...

- Would you like another suggestion from me?

ACTION

Purpose

1. To carry out a purposeful and specific action taken to move away from the Present Position in a measurable degree which will provide momentum for continuing the journey towards the objective.
2. To promote confidence and self-belief in the performer by focusing on taking one positive step, without distraction.

3. To challenge and enhance the external perception of the abilities and potential of the performer.
4. To establish a supportive relationship (connection) between performer and others (e.g. boss or team) that will encourage activity in new and challenging arenas.
5. To identify any obstacles including lack of confidence that may prevent the agreed action taking place and defining an alternative preliminary tactic.
6. To agree a time scale for action and a time for review in which the learning and personal growth of the performer is evaluated as well as the progress of the particular task or activity.
7. To ensure that the agreed action has an irrevocable commitment which can be modified only by subsequent agreement if absolutely necessary.
8. For the leader, colleague or boss to feel "in control" by knowing that the performer is aware of all issues and is committed to taking an agreed action – and the performer feels "in control" because he/she feels there is organisational support for the action of their choice.

Tips

1. Better a small action that gets delivered than a big promise that doesn't! A small action can be reviewed within a short time-frame and the "pace" can be stepped up later.
2. Always let the performer go with their choice where possible. They will put more passion and energy into it. Just check it's roughly in the appropriate direction. Any serious deviation will quickly get picked up in the review.

3. By setting up the conversation in the meeting to be about the performer's promise to take the performer's choice of action towards the performer's objective, with your agreed support, you have framed your relationship. Follow-up support and subsequent reviews are referenced back to the original commitment. Authoritarian rebukes, if applied, will not cause anger or distress whereas in a traditional framework they probably would, if only in silence!

4. Refer to the ultimate objective as a constant source of inspiration. If it doesn't inspire it's the wrong objective!

5. Make sure the first action takes place within say, two weeks. The impetus will have gone if it's delayed.

6. Check the level of confidence. If below a 9 out of 10, explore the reasons and unearth the obstacle. Then focus on overcoming the obstacle as the first action step (e.g. "Before I hold that meeting I want to do some research first – then I'll feel more confident about the meeting." The research is now the new first action). Check the degree of commitment to taking the action. This is not their evaluation of whether the action will produce the result they want. It's simply "Are you going to do it – whatever the result you get?" If commitment is less that a 9 (some people never volunteer a 10), dig out the obstacle and focus on that. You may feel you have gone one step backwards but you will very quickly move forwards faster.

7. Make sure you absolutely believe they are going to carry out their agreement to action. Your belief will affect their belief and boost it. If you don't believe it, they won't either. Go back to Objectives and choose a smaller step.

Questions to ask:

- What are you going to do first? By when?
- What obstacles might stop you?
- What will you do to overcome them?
- How confident are you (0–10)?
- What support do you need?
- What will you do to get that support?
- How can I support you?
- What is your commitment to this action (0–10)?
- When will we meet to review?

Questions raise awareness. They help to get to the truth. Only from truth can the best decisions be made. These can generate the responsibility for action so that personal and team growth is constantly developing.

Here are some examples of where questions create their own model, or agenda, to structure effective communication and increase the likelihood of achieving the results you want:

- a presentation format for communicating information and ideas.

QUESTIONS RAISE AWARENESS

- a selling and influencing model for opening up discussions with others in the organisation.
- a guide for your own appraisals giving you more influence and control to present your perspective of yourself and your performance.
- a self-coaching "aide- memoire".
- a questionnaire for teams.
- the basis for an appraisal by the appraiser.
- a tool for self-managed teams.

Printed in the United States
by Baker & Taylor Publisher Services